LOVING TO FIGHT

OR

FIGHTING TO LOVE?

Winning the *Spiritual* Battle for Your Marriage

by Gordon Dalbey
with Mary Andrews-Dalbey

Copyright

Loving to Fight or Fighting to Love? Winning the Spiritual Battle for Your Marriage

© Copyright 2017 - Gordon Dalbey & Mary Andrews-Dalbey, PhD

ISBN # 978-0-692-98399-7

Published by Civitas Press, LLC

San Jose, CA

www.civitaspress.com

I ask the God of our Lord Jesus Christ, the glorious Father, to give you the Spirit, who will make you wise and reveal God to you, so that you will know him. I ask that your minds may be opened to see his light, so that you will know what is the hope to which he has called you, how rich are the wonderful blessings he promises his people, and how very great is his power at work in us who believe. This power working in us is the same as the mighty strength which he used when he raised Christ from death and seated him at his right side in the heavenly world. Ephes. 1:15-20

OTHER BOOKS
BY GORDON DALBEY

Healing the Masculine Soul
How God Restores Men to Real Manhood

Sons of the Father
Healing the Father-Wound in Men Today

Fight like a Man
A New Warrior for a New Warfare

Do Pirates Wear Pajamas?
and other Mysteries in the Adventure of Fathering

Broken by Religion, Healed by God
*Restoring the Evangelical, Sacramental,
Pentecostal, Social Justice Church*

No Small Snakes
A Journey into Spiritual Warfare

Religion vs. Reality
Facing the Home Front in Spiritual Warfare

Pure Sex
The Spirituality of Desire

A Couples' Guide to Spiritual Warfare
Deliverance Ministry for Marriages

**Gordon Dalbey and Mary Andrews-Dalbey may be contacted
for speaking engagements and other resources at
Box 61042, Santa Barbara, CA 93160
www.abbafather.com**

The question is not Who's right? but
What's God trying to teach us?

Forgive us, Father, for turning away from each other
instead of turning toward you.

Anger is often pain masquerading as power.

The image of God is male and female together;
that's why the enemy of God wants to destroy marriages.

It's not about making your marriage work, but
letting God work in your marriage.

God does not lift up one partner to humble the other;
He lifts up Himself to humble you both.

With the capacity to judge,
it's not far from Paradise to a fight.

Sexual intimacy happens not by trying harder,
but by surrendering more deeply to God and each other.

Love blesses a wife's womanhood;
Respect blesses a husband's manhood.

Great love calls for great courage—
and great faith in the One who animates it.

Money exposes your values;
that's why it's such an explosive issue for marriages.

Jesus loves your children because, like Him,
they restore innocence to an awfully guilty world—even your own.

Desperation is solid currency in the Kingdom of God.

Faith is not righteously giving control to God,
but humbly confessing that you never had control.

When it's harder to stay up than to make up,
you're ready to grow up.

When you let Jesus heal your childhood wounds,
you don't need to act them out any more in your marriage.

"That was scary!" my kindergartner son exclaimed, beaming with excitement as I finished our bedtime story. And then strangely, he knit his brow.

"Daddy, how come all your adventures happened before you knew Mommy?"

Hesitating, I smiled. "Well, son...," I allowed, bending over to tuck him in, "hunting crocodiles in Nigeria and facing those bears in the Sierra mountains was sure scary, alright—and fun! But actually, my scariest and most fun adventure stories have happened since I met Mommy. Maybe someday I'll tell you one of them."

Maybe someday, I thought to myself as I hugged him goodnight, *I'll even write a book about it.*

Contents

Foreword   9

Introduction   13

1   Finding Your Voice: *Starting Apart, Finishing Together*   23

2   In the Beginning: *Why It's So Hard*   35

3   Never Waste a Good Fight: *Getting a Third Opinion from the Great Physician*   53

4   For Better or Worse: *Letting Go of Judgments*   67

5   When You're Hot, You're Hot; When You're Not… *It's Time to Talk about Sex*   90

6   Hurt People Hurt People, *But Holy Spirit Heals*   111

7   Leaving Father and Mother: *The Trailhead to Marriage*   122

8   For Richer or Poorer: *Whose Money Is It?*   139

9   Staying Focused as Parents: *Whose Child Is It?*   152

10   Fire Prevention: *How to Stop a Fight before It Starts*   174

11   Caution! I Love Like You: *The Case for Grace*   205

Afterword   219

About the Authors   222

NOTES   231

> Funny, what a quarrel can do
> After so many thrills;
> We have wrecked in a moment
> What has taken us a lifetime to build.
> So Darlin' please, come on home.
>
> "Come Home," song by Barbara Lewis[1]

It was the Fight of fights
And yet...

Foreword

Everything that happens in this world happens at the time God chooses.... He sets the time for sorrow and the time for joy. The time for mourning and the time for dancing, the time for making love and the time for not making love, the time for kissing and the time for not kissing. Eccles. 3:1,4,5

It was the Fight of fights.

Tempers blazed.

Fingers pointed.

Accusations flew.

Shouts fired.

Threats launched.

Feet dug in.

Positions defended.

No prisoners taken.

"You never...!"

"You always...!"

"I'm done!"

"Fine! I'm out of here!"

One leaves for a friend's house that night.

And then the silence. The confident standoff.

Let's see who blinks first!

The sun sets on anger.

Shadows fall on distant, self-satisfied pillows

and eyes that do not close.

No problem.

At first.

Then the sleepless justification. Self-assuring mental re-hash. Re-enforced defenses. Sharpened barbs. A new zinger determined to fire next time.

Stomachs churn.

The Accuser smirks.

Righteously alone, the accusers examine their bedroom ceilings, anticipating.

But no call comes.

So what? I'm right. I won the argument.

Until at last, seeping relentlessly through the darkness, comes the fear of losing.

Everything.

What if we never...?

Later the next evening, as husband and wife lie smiling in each other's arms, they turn to each other with a kiss and....

What? Hold on!

What is this, some kind of sadistic fairy tale? We're talking knock-down, drag-'em-out brawl, and suddenly they're making love?

How in the world did that happen?

I'm glad you asked.

They say marriages are made in heaven.

So are thunder and lightning.

--Clint Eastwood[2]

> The problem in Christian marriages today is not that our faith is a flawed belief system. Rather, human nature is a flawed condition, which has blinded us to Jesus and His power to heal.

Introduction

> *I know that good does not live in me—that is in my human nature. For even though the desire to do good is in me, I am not able to do it. I don't do the good I want to do; instead, I do the evil I do not want to do.... Who will rescue me from this body that is taking me to death?*
> Romans 7:18,24

AS MARY AND I were holding each other gratefully after the above argument, we praised God for delivering us through the battle into yet deeper love for each other. Before long, it struck us both: How many couples, we wondered, never make it through such battles? How many marriages set sail filled with wedding promises and honeymoon joy, only to break apart later on the unyielding rocks amid storms like our own?

Mary and I are both highly educated people, with six college degrees between us. What's more, we're trained in relationship dynamics. She's a psychologist and I'm an ordained minister and writer of books on the subject. Neither of us is an abuser, addict, or adulterer. Yet all our years of education, professional training, and virtue had not saved us either from our conflict or its potential damage.

Maybe you just don't understand all the fuss about couples' fighting. Maybe you and your spouse never yell at each other or refuse to talk. Maybe you never even have a disagreement, and if you do, you always talk about it openly and settle things calmly.

But if your Marriage Richter Scale ever registers somewhere between shouting and stony silence, welcome.

Read on.

At the outset, I need to say here that if you're dealing in your marriage with physical abuse, addiction, or adultery, get professional help immediately. Many resources are available for these problems, which must be confronted in order to "fight fair" together. Even as a book about jogging may not be immediately helpful to someone with a broken leg, this book will be most effective after you've begun dealing deliberately with such overriding issues.

"You can't argue with a bottle," as the spouse of an alcoholic once said to me.

BATTLE AGAINST MARRIAGES

In fact, the divorce rate among Christians is about the same as among others. The statistics are debated, but according to the Barna Research Group, 33% of Americans have been divorced; among Christians, 34% of Protestants and 28% of Catholics.[3] My ministry experience over the years suggests that the other two thirds of Christian marriages are not always 100% healthy and happy.

While church leaders often lament those statistics and may speak shame upon divorce, clearly Christianity's uniqueness is not widely evident in marriages today. Whatever overcoming power God has offered specifically to His Church is therefore not being received and exercised by many, if not most Christian couples.

Why not? What, in fact, is that uniqueness to Christianity? How can husbands and wives appropriate its power to heal and restore their relationships?

Why, indeed, is the battle against marriage so fierce? What's so important to God's purposes in marriage that draws such flak from His enemy? How can we fight with God against those attacks and cooperate with Him to fulfill those purposes?

These questions are tough, but essential amid the pain and disappointment in marriages today. Without answers, it's tempting to join church dropouts who conclude that Christianity is just not up to the task.

I can understand that from personal experience.

In the mid-1980's, I went through a divorce myself after three years of seminary and eight years of pastoring a church. By the grace of God, the shame, discouragement, and pain of that experience drove me not angrily away from Christianity, but rather, desperately after a more real and more powerful relationship with Jesus than my church background had afforded me (see my books *No Small Snakes: A Journey into Spiritual Warfare* and *Broken by Religion, Healed by God*).

In my journey, I discovered that the problem in Christian marriages today is not that our faith is a flawed belief system, but rather, that human nature is a flawed condition. Since our wedding in 1990, Mary and I have experienced not only that flaw in each of us, but also the power of God to overcome it.

The Good News is that, via His Spirit, God is actively present in Christian marriages today, even—if not especially—in our conflicts. Mary and I know that's true, both from God's word in the Bible and from painful but blessed experience which has confirmed it.

ANCIENT WITNESS

Indeed, that ancient written witness has encouraged us to cry out to Father God even today for His saving hand in our life together. In that process, we've seen Him overcome our self-centeredness and heal wounding in our marriage as well as in many others.

"Thank God for God!" we like to say after we've given up on ourselves and allowed Him to do that.

Like surgery, it's no picnic—but it does bring healing. Along with the biblical witness, we can testify that in fact, "this power working in us is the same as the mighty strength which he used when he raised Christ from death" (Ephes. 1: 20). Education, relationship techniques, conflict resolution therapies, and the like can be helpful resources in fighting for a marriage, whether Christian or not. In the midst of a battle, however, Mary and I have found that nothing substitutes for knowing that the Commander-in-Chief of God's armies has not only defeated the enemy of you both, but stands with you in His victory.

"Remember that I have commanded you to be determined and confident," as He exhorted when Israel faced the forbidding walls of Jericho upon entering the Promised Land. "Do not be afraid or discouraged, for I, the Lord your God, am with you wherever you go" (Joshua 1:9).

That Scripture should be read at every Christian wedding.

To portray the difficulties in marriages today, I deliberately choose military terms here such as "attack," "fight," and "battle"—not simply as cheap tabloid images to grab your attention, but to reflect a palpable reality. Any Christian couple who have struggled for healing together during—and after—a quarrel know that such warfare terms are naturally as well as biblically apt.

Occasionally, therefore, I'll refer here to the "enemy" of God and associated "spirits"—that is, negative spiritual entities as portrayed in the Bible—and "deliverance," as the process of being set free from their power and influence. This book focuses on the basic issues and attitudes which must be dealt with first, in order to minister deliverance effectively.

For husbands and wives who feel ready to delve more deliberately into that ministry, I've written a smaller companion to this book, *A Couples' Guide to Spiritual Warfare*. In addition, my personal story *No Small Snakes: A Journey into Spiritual Warfare* offers a larger, comprehensive view of the subject.

MARRIED OR UN-DIVORCED?

In any case, too many Christian couples today are fighting a lonely battle to survive together, at best "for the kids' sake." To these struggling husbands and wives, "married" can simply mean "un-divorced."

Too often, Christians don't tell others about our problems, for fear of being judged and shamed. Desperately, we can pray, read our bibles, go to church, tithe, and do everything that's apparently required to win God's favor—while the fighting and hurting continue at home (see "The Wolf Loves the Lone Sheep" in *Sons of the Father: Healing the Father-Wound in Men Today*).

Walking in God's healing, meanwhile, is a step beyond walking in His favor. In fact, we already have His overwhelming favor in Jesus, via His active presence today in Holy Spirit. This book is based on Mary's and my experience that the Great Physician revealed in Jesus *wants* to heal us, even as a good father wants to bless his son and daughter (see Matt. 8:2-3).

The only question is, Will we get up on the operating table and let Him?

That is, will we refuse to let shame blackmail us—even as Adam and Eve—into hiding from God and each other? (see "Blackmailed by Shame" in *Broken by Religion, Healed by God*).

When we yield to shame, the voice of religion mocks our cry for help by demanding, "Will you try harder to please God?"

When we look beyond our shame to Father God and His overwhelming grace, we can hear Jesus pleading instead, "Will the Son of Man find faith on earth when He comes?" (Luke 18:8).

Faith amid conflicts doesn't mean gritting your teeth and striving to conjure up deeper trust. Nor does it mean pulling the covers over your head and ignoring your problems.

Rather, a vital faith grows amid the terrifying, renewing, often self-obliterating process of surrendering to the Father of you both. It means trusting Him to use even your deepest brokenness to draw you closer to Him and to each other, and thereby to prepare you for His larger purposes together.

The Kingdom rule of God in your life is not about what you achieve, but Whom you receive.

GETTING REAL

Trying to win God's favor is about your performance, and not His. Sooner or later, honest couples confess that their human wisdom and strength is never enough to merit God's favor. That revelation allows them at last to surrender to Him and cry out with the Apostle Paul, "Who will rescue me from this body that is taking me to death?"

Getting real like that before God and each other allows you to experience the grace in Paul's answer: "Thanks be to God, who does this through our Lord Jesus Christ" (Rom. 7:24,25).

That's the Good News which our faith proclaims—and which God's Holy Spirit enables.

Sure, Mary and I have discovered that our worldly expertise can be helpful in a quarrel to clarify the issue. But it has no power in itself to heal the wound which started the fight, nor to deliver us from the sin-nature in both of us which continued it.

The defining question for Christian couples, therefore, is not How can we make our marriage work?, but rather, *How can we let God work in our marriage?*

That's what this book is about.

After the "Fight of fights" described above, Mary and I marveled at God's leading us through it to deeper understanding and healing together. Indeed, we were struck by a sense not only of humility, but also of such gratitude that we wanted to help other couples benefit from our experience (see 2 Corinth. 1:1-5).

That's how this book was conceived.

At first, we balked. Sure, it's great to help others in trouble. But in order to be effective in this sensitive, even volatile arena of husband-wife conflict, clearly we'd need to get real. That means sharing our own sins and mistakes, and thereby risking judgment and shame among fellow Christians.

MARRIAGE GLASS HALF FULL

The fact that you're reading these words here tells you that we decided our marriage glass is half-full, not half-empty. This book, therefore, does not focus primarily on our shortcomings—genuine and dismaying as they've been, and can still be—but rather, on the Father's amazing grace to redeem them for His greater plans.

In the end, therefore, our personal fears of exposure were trumped by an utter dependence upon Father God for our life together, a determination to receive the overcoming power Jesus lived and died to give us, and a desire for Holy Spirit to work fully in Christian marriages today.

Without this dynamic Trinity at work in our lives, the two of us would not even be alive today, much less married to each other (see my personal birth story "Delivered from Abortion" in *Religion vs Reality: Facing the Home Front in Spiritual Warfare*). With that confession, we find freedom in Paul's promise,

> I tried keeping the rules and working my head off to please God, and it didn't work. So I quit being a "law man" so that I could be *God's* man. Christ's life showed me how, *and enabled me to do it.* I identified myself completely with him. Indeed, I have been crucified with Christ. *My ego is no longer central.* It is no longer important that I appear righteous before you or have your good opinion, and I am no longer driven to impress God. Christ lives in me. The life you see me living is not "mine," but *it is lived by faith in the Son of God,* who loved me and gave himself for me. *I am not going back on that.* (Galat. 2:19-21 *The Message Bible* italics mine)

Paul's attitude or orientation here applies directly to Christian husbands and wives. Victory in the spiritual battle for your marriage is not about "appearing righteous," upholding your ego, and winning the argument. It's about releasing that self-serving charade to Jesus and nailing it to the cross with Him—and thereby, receiving humbly the power of His Spirit to raise you both up.

When you're fighting each other and the enemy comes calling for your marriage, being Jesus-centered allows you to tell the self-centered powers of the world, "Sorry, but you're too late. We have nothing left to give you. We've already given ourselves and our marriage to Jesus."

Such surrendered faith allows you to turn from looking angrily into each other's eyes to looking humbly and hopefully into Jesus' eyes. "Forgive us, Father," you can say at last, "for not trusting your power to save us and *for turning away from each other instead of turning toward you.*"

When you've given up on yourself, that is, there's nothing of yourself left to lose—and freedom for God to gain more territory in your heart. Your ego is "no longer central." It's not about saving face, but revealing God's face; not about photo-shopping your image, but promoting the reality of God's image—which is, in fact, "male and female *together*" (Gen. 1:27 italics mine).

A PROCESS

This faith and life-surrendering humility describes what the Father has been growing in Mary and me—even, indeed precisely, through our conflicts. In that process, we've discovered that marriage, like life, is an upending journey of trusting God and giving up our agendas to Him. That's how His agendas become more clear to us and His power to fulfill them more accessible.

The key word here is "process." We're certainly not wholly there yet, nor expect to be until the Lord returns. *But we know that life abides in that walk*—from experience so painful, so real, so fearful, and yet so promising that we've determined like Paul that we're "not going back on that."

We can't ever reach the stars, as the old saying goes, but we set our course by them.

And so, with a nod to our not-yet-fully-redeemed human nature, I submitted this new book idea to my Intercessors' Platoon for discernment.

"I know you're onto something and God is in it," one brother emailed me back immediately. "I just hung up the phone after a conversation where I learned that a newlywed Christian couple we know is having troubles. They have no family support network and no training to deal with their conflicts. Both come from divorced parents.

"So many Christian marriages we know—new and long-time—are struggling. If we, the church, are serious about solving this growing problem, we need to be deliberate about providing on-going mentoring beyond the honeymoon. The insanity of thinking we don't need any more help once we're married and can heal ourselves is horrific."

My intercessor then seized me with two final words:

"Write fast."

> The man and the woman must each find his/her own voice before they can communicate together with mutual respect.

1

Finding Your Voice

Starting Apart, Finishing Together

> *Don't, by the way, read too much into the differences here between men and women. Neither man nor woman can go it alone or claim priority.... The first woman came from man, true—but ever since then, every man comes from a woman! And since virtually everything comes from God anyway, let's quit going through these "who's first" routines.*
> 1 Corinth. 11:11 TMB

A FEW YEARS AGO, a young businessman on the East Coast founded a thriving men's ministry based on my book *Fight like a Man: A New Manhood for a New Warfare*. One day, he called me frustrated by what

I believe marks the growing edge of God's work between men and women today.

"Our leaders have been going through your books and material for some time now and it's been great," he told me. "We've gotten real with each other as men, talked about everything from our dads and kids to jobs and sex. We've learned to know God as our Father and seen major healing and deliverance together. I don't think any of us has ever known brotherhood and fellowship like we've got here now."

He paused in frustration. "The more secure we men get with each other and the Father, the more we want to move out into spiritual warfare. But we're realizing we can't go there without our wives on board. In fact, we really don't want to. What we want now is to be battle partners together with them.

"The women see we're getting healed," he explained, "and they want that for us. But at the same time, they're starting to feel left out and angry. We men are getting stronger, but our wives seem afraid of our strength and don't trust us to use it for them instead of against them. We don't want to misuse it, but we've worked hard to get what we have now and don't want to lose it.

"As men, we're not sure what to do," he confessed. "We started this ministry because we wanted to get somewhere that none of our fathers—not even our churches—could take us. A lot of it began with just wanting to be good husbands and fathers, which means getting along better with our wives.

"It seems like we've come as far now as we can go without the women alongside us."

He sighed, uncertain. "So we were wondering if maybe your wife Mary could come out here with you and meet with the women while you meet with us men, and see if somehow as husbands and wives we can work this through together?"

Immediately, I told this brother how much I respected his and the other men's determination to become better husbands and fathers. I said they reminded me, in fact, of Paul's heart for the church at Thessalonica:

> We always thank God for you all and always mention you in our prayers. For we remember before our God and Father how you put your faith into practice, how your love made you work so hard, and how your hope in our Lord Jesus Christ is firm. (1 Thess. 1:2,3)

With that, I assured him that Mary and I would be honored to help.

BATTLE IS ON

The weekend he suggested was perfect, as our 14-year-old son would be leaving the country then on his church's high school mission trip to the South Pacific in Fiji. I went online to book our flight for the morning after his—and immediately the battle was on. When I clicked "Purchase," the airlines site page suddenly went down and then came back up—at $300 per ticket more. Four hours on the phone with an airlines agent finally restored the original price.

Then a few days later, I was startled when the couples' weekend host forwarded me an email signed by several wives threatening to boycott. "We won't come to another event telling us to submit to our husbands!" they declared.

I never saw that one coming. Suddenly, our couples' event took off—at warp speed!

Father, help! I cried out, not without fear and trembling. *What did we get ourselves in for?*

Clearly, this was not about to be as straightforward as my men's events! Uneasy, I forwarded the email to Mary, suggesting gingerly that maybe she might want to reply to the sisters' concern?

"I like these women already!" Mary exclaimed when I went into her study to talk about it.

Sensing my discomfort if not alarm, she smiled. "Don't worry," she assured. "I'm going tell both the men and women to 'submit to one another out of reverence for Christ' (Ephes. 5:21). I'm going to help the women trust and respect their husbands as partners. But first, they need to discover their identity and strength as daughters of the Father."

Mary sent this reply to the women's email, and with her reassurance, they agreed to the event. At that, the host's wisdom in asking Mary to come with me was confirmed; with a prayer of trust and surrender, we began packing.

The day before our flight, we put our son on a bus with his youth group to Los Angeles airport, about 100 miles south of us, then rushed to get ready for our next day's cross-country flight in the other direction. That afternoon, however, shortly before his flight across the Pacific to Fiji, our son called desperately from L.A. airport. The airlines, he said, wouldn't let him board the plane because his passport—inadvertently washed with his jeans—was separated slightly at the cover.

Immediately, I drove to our local Post Office, where the Passport clerk, a friend and Christian, said it all: "There's nothing we can do but pray."

As we prayed there in the Post Office passport room, my son called my cell phone again to say the airlines had agreed to fly him to Fiji. I had barely sighed in relief when he added that they would have to fly him back to L.A. immediately if the security officials in Fiji wouldn't accept his passport.

Frantically, I called a friend in L.A. and asked if our son could call for help should that happen and he get stuck there when we were out of town? "Sure," my friend said; immediately, I called my son and gave him my friend's phone number, then dashed home to pray with Mary.

Afterward, I emailed our conference host back East.

YOU GOT WARFARE

"You want spiritual warfare?" I wrote. "You got it. Call everybody there and pray to release our family." Determined to proceed with the couples' conference, with an uneasy sigh and a prayer Mary and I surrendered our son and his dilemma to the Father and went ahead with our plans.

Father, give us faith for this! we cried out together.

Warfare, indeed. At the airport the next morning, the check-in agent typed in our tickets, then frowned in confusion. "You have reservations alright," he noted, "—but we don't have seats for you."

Exasperated, I urged him to keep trying, and he returned to his keyboard while Mary and I stood hand-in-hand, glancing uneasily at the clock and praying fiercely under our breath.

At last, five minutes before the flight, he tossed us two tickets: "Run over to the gate and see if you can get on."

We rushed over, carry-ons and all.

"I'm sorry," the gate agent declared, "but we only have one seat. You'll have to split up."

At once, I insisted on our two seats. "That's not acceptable," I declared, panting after our sprint and straining for a composed voice. "We need to get on this flight together."

As the agent turned back to his computer, Mary and I held hands and prayed again quietly. And then, I understood: Our trip was about reconciling men and women, and the enemy was scheming to separate Mary and me at the outset.

A minute later, the clicking of the agent's keyboard stopped. "Looks like we have your seats after all," he declared, raising his eyebrows in surprise.

We never paused to ask him how that happened; we just grabbed our tickets and dashed out across the tarmac to the plane. Exhausted but thankful, we fell into our seats and praised God just as the flight attendant pulled the cabin door shut.

When we landed at our destination, our suitcases and book table materials were nowhere to be found, and didn't turn up until two days later. We didn't know whether our son had made it to Fiji or had been sent back to L.A., a hundred miles from our empty home with no way to get there. We could only release it all to the Father—and keep going in our rumpled travel clothes.

That night, Mary met with fifteen wives at the host's home. I met with the husbands, all from several local churches, at the men's ministry center they had together leased and built out—including rooms for weightlifting, computer terminals, counseling, cooking, and larger meetings.

"The women came in guarded and resistant," Mary told me later. "They were carrying so much emotion—I just encouraged them to share their fears and concerns before saying anything at all myself."

Meanwhile, I spoke to the men about how to battle for, and not against a woman, from my chapter "The Woman as Ally" in *Fight like a Man*. Two hours later, at 10 pm, the men's session was finished.

"Go ahead and call Mary!" the leader urged me with a smile. "Let's see if the women are ready to meet with us." Turning to the Men's Center land line, he lifted up the phone expectantly and handed it to me. "I'll just put on the speaker phone so we can all listen in together here and feel closer to our wives!"

Murmurs of approval spread across the room as the men sat up excitedly.

Buoyed by the fellowship of brothers and their enthusiasm, I called Mary. "The men are all finished with our session!" I exclaimed when she answered. "In fact, all of us here are listening in to this call on the speaker system. Are the women done yet?"

Hearing my words over the amplified phone, the men hushed and leaned forward.

"*Done?*" Mary burst out, her exasperation echoing off the weight room window. "I only began teaching a minute ago. It's taken two hours just for the women to vent their feelings!"

A distinct sense of masculine uneasiness spread across the room. Cautiously, the men exhaled and eased back into their seats, confused.

Clearly, this was not going according to plan.

NOT OUR PLAN

At least, not our plan.

"Well…," I offered tentatively, "I mean, like, … are they ready to meet with us men, at least tomorrow morning over here at the men's center?"

A determined sigh sounded forth from the speaker phone as Mary hesitated. "OK," she allowed. "I'll ask the women—and I'll hold out my phone here so you and all the other men there can hear what they say."

The men leaned forward again, now tensely.

After a moment, we heard Mary announce to the women, "The men are listening on the speaker phone. They want to know if we're ready to meet with them tomorrow morning?"

"NOOO! NOOO! *NO!*" a determined chorus of distinctly feminine discontent burst out.

Raucous background cries and clatter rang out as Mary turned back to her phone. "Tell the men we need a little more time," she advised graciously.

"Well,…OK….," I managed, glancing uncertain from the speaker phone to the men, now shifting warily. "So…, thanks, Honey. Oh… kay… I mean, I'll talk to you later."

Slowly, I hung up and turned to the men—whose expectant smiles and murmurs had now given way to frowns and heavy silence.

With a shrug of surrender, I exhaled and smiled thinly. "Well, men," I offered, "how about this for adventure? Looks like we got more than we bargained for! We're in unknown territory, and I might add, a little scared. But hey, we're in it together as brothers!"

At last, tentative but good-natured laughter broke out across the room.

Clearly, the women were finding their voice at last and bonding together themselves—even as the men had done in their own previous meetings together. I led a brief prayer encouraging the brothers, blessing the sisters, and surrendering our control to the Father. Then I released the men.

The next morning, again at our separate venues, Mary talked to the women about grounding their identity in Christ and how childhood wounds from Mom and Dad can sabotage intimacy with a man. She then led them in healing and forgiveness prayers. I talked to the men about overcoming our fear of women, as often rooted in the mother-wound (see "Cutting the Cord: A Second Post-Partum" in *Sons of the Father*).

THE FATHER'S GRACE

The men had planned an upscale catered lunch in the women's behalf. At noon, I called Mary from the Men's Center again and at last, the women agreed to come together with us. Among the men, a collective sigh of masculine relief burst forth.

Later, as the women arrived at the Center, Mary entered first and looked at me from across the room, her head shaking slowly with a mixture of wonder and exhaustion. Immediately, I went to hug her, and told her how much the men and I appreciated what she had done. After a moment, she and I turned to see the other women coming in—and were awed by the Father's grace as couples paused tentatively, then embraced warmly and sat holding each other at the tables.

That afternoon, as husbands and wives sat arm-in-arm before us, Mary and I took turns teaching more specifically on spiritual warfare and lessons we've learned as a couple in keeping the enemy from drawing us apart. We closed by praying over the group, and broke several major stronghold spirits—including "independence" and "division," which we sensed had been attacking many of the marriages there.

"Neither man nor woman can go it alone or claim priority," I read from 1 Corinth. 11:11-12 (TMB):

> The first woman came from a man, true—
> but ever since then, every man comes from a
> woman! And since virtually everything comes
> from God anyway, let's quit going through
> these 'who's first' routines.

Later that night, as we stepped into our hotel room to rest at last, I sighed in relief—and was startled as Mary suddenly collapsed onto the bed with an "awful headache." We realized in that moment how significant Mary's ministry had been, essentially to broker the peace which Father God had planned for the couples.

For over an hour, we prayed fiercely in the Spirit against this enemy backlash at her via spirits of woman-hating, destruction, and others. We then asked for the blood of Jesus to cleanse her from all effects of those spirits and praised Jesus, until she finally was able to sleep.

Thankfully, Mary awoke refreshed. During the next afternoon's session break, we received an email at last from the youth group director in Fiji, saying that our son had passed through customs OK and was enjoying his mission work there.

"Haleluia!" the men and women shouted at the announcement—along with Dad and Mom!

The next day, we arrived back home in Santa Barbara exhausted, but uplifted—only to find that yet again, our luggage was lost. After two frustrating days of talking with officials, I finally gave up on the airlines, and in the name of Jesus commanded that our bags be released.

That afternoon, an agent called. "We have your bags!" she reassured.

At last! I thought. *Thank you, Lord!*

"They're right here in Yuma anytime you want to come and pick them up."

"*Yuma*, like in Arizona?" I exclaimed. As anger stirred within me, suddenly the sheer buffoonery of it all broke through and overwhelmed me with a laugh—and humble repentance.

BATTLE LESSONS

The Father, I realized as so many times before, has a sense of humor—and was inviting me to share in it.

At last, I knew. With so many frustrations, the enemy had been trying to steal our energies and distract us from Father God's healing work. Rather than cower in the face of such strikes, He was ridiculing the enemy's frantic efforts.

Politely, I thanked the agent for calling, then asked her please to return our bags to us here in Santa Barbara, California.

I hung up and fell on my knees in thanksgiving, praising the Father for our weekend adventure—and its lessons.

We learned first that, in order for men and women to walk side by side in the journey of reconciliation, you can only respect the other's walk insofar as you respect your own. Thus, this unsettling, but essential lesson of healthy love: *You can stand together with your spouse only insofar as you can stand apart from each other with your Father God.*

Thus, the men's group secured the husbands' identity, which led them to want that security for their wives. That stirred them to arrange the women's gathering with Mary, which culminated in the husbands' and wives' coming together.

Deliberately, responsibly, we begin apart.

Faithfully, victoriously, we press on together.

What's more, we learned that *the intensity of the fight often measures the significance of the victory.* In fact, I believe our fierce battle that weekend points to a much larger contest—basic, in fact, to natural origins and divine destiny.

"How can we reconcile races, nations, or any other larger human differences," as Rev. Susan Miele has noted, "if we can't reconcile with the other half of ourselves?"—that is, with the most primary, indeed the very Genesis of human differences, in man and woman?[4]

In fact, could God's desire to reconcile humanity to Himself be rooted in the separation of Eve from Adam and the fig leaves that followed?

My son,
This is the woman I have chosen
for you to love.
My daughter,
This is the man I have chosen
for you to love.
"Thank you, Father," they said,
"—but why is it so hard?"

> Our spiritual enemy's most deliberate efforts to misrepresent God focus on His most basic reflection in this world—namely, the union of male and female.

2

In the Beginning

Why It's So Hard

So God created man in his own image, in the image of God he created him, male and female he created them.

God blessed them and said to them, "be fruitful and increase in number...."
Gen. 1:27,28NIV

IN ORDER TO CONCEIVE a child—to "be fruitful and increase in number" as God intends—something specific, unique, and essential to both the man and the woman is required. In fact, the very image or "nature" of God (TMB) is reflected in the union of man and woman. Through their ultimate union in sexual intercourse, the Creator thereby produces His finest work, namely, a new human being.

The enemy of God, however, does not want Him to be genuinely known. In fact, that's the work of Holy Spirit, "who will make you wise and reveal God to you, so that you will know him" (Ephes. 1:15).

Since the Evil One cannot deceive, destroy, or otherwise restrain God, its best shot is to spread lies about Him. Hence, the title "father of Lies" (John 8:44). For so, at the very beginning of life, Eve tells the Snake that God said she and Adam would die if they ate from the Tree of Knowledge.

"That's not true," the Snake scoffs. "God said that because He knows that if you eat from it you will be like God, and know what is good and what is bad" (Gen. 3:4,5). The enemy thereby misrepresents God as a jealous egomaniac, in order to keep Him from being known genuinely, that is, as *a loving Father who sets boundaries for His children's protection.*

The enemy's most deliberate efforts to distort the divine image therefore focus on God's most fundamental reflection in this world— namely, on the union of "male and female." The most determined attacks against knowing God will thereby aim at distorting sexuality and sabotaging Godly union of man and woman—even casting the two as enemies rather than mutual components of God's image.

Thus, the expression, "the war between the sexes."

Let's be clear about this: There is no war between the sexes. Rather, there's a *self-centered sin-nature in both men and women, and a spiritual enemy who leverages that to divide and pit us against each other.*

Thus, God's perspective reveals the so-called "war between the sexes" as a wordly sham. It's *an unholy distraction from the true war against marriages, hosted by the enemy of God.*

Marriage, therefore, is not just some moral agenda, social decorum, or religious ordinance. Insofar as it comprises the image of God, it's in the nature of the Creator, and thereby, of His created universe. It's basic to knowing God and to embracing His purposes for humanity.

That's why God is impelled to create and uphold marriages. But it's also why the enemy of God is literally hell-bent to destroy marriages, both individually in homes and collectively as an institution.

Put it another way: the character of God is revealed primarily and most authentically in the union of man and woman. No other contender comes close in significance—neither nature's grandeur, acts of kindness, artistic excellence, moral standards, religious creeds, nor philosophical ideals. None of these can produce a new human being and is therefore essential to humanity.

The fact that we would presume any other such contender at all simply reveals our fear of sexuality for the lack of control which it reveals (see "Controlling Uncontrollable Desire" in *Pure Sex: The Spirituality of Desire*).

SEXUAL REVOLUTION

In "Judaism's Sexual Revolution," [5] Jewish author Dennis Prager offers a compelling historical perspective. Judaism, he notes, first appeared thousands of years ago in a world where virtually all forms of sexual expression were tolerated if not affirmed.

In fact, the "sexual revolution" that Judaism initiated so long ago was not anything-goes hedonism—which, unlike our smug misconception today, is not at all "modern," but altogether ancient. Rather, Judaism instituted the radical concept that sexual expression is by its nature designed for, and thereby aptly limited to male-female relationship covenanted before God.

"In order to become fully human," Prager explains, "male and female must join":

> In the words of Genesis, "God created the
> human, ... male and female He created them."

> The union of male and female is not merely
> some lovely ideal; it is the essence of the
> Jewish outlook on becoming human. To deny
> it is tantamount to denying a primary purpose
> of life....

The effects of this ancient "sexual revolution," he concludes, are foundational to civilization today as we know it—and thereby, to its survival:

> At stake is our civilization. It is very easy
> to forget what Judaism has wrought and what
> Christians have created in the West.... The
> bedrock of this civilization, and of Jewish life,
> has been the centrality and purity of family life.

That's why families are under such spiritual attack in our time.

In the next chapter, I'll tell the story of how Mary and I first learned to fight as partners with God to overcome such attacks on our own marriage. In order to appreciate our story, however, you need first to understand how our human sin-nature has historically distorted God's image in man and woman together.

FATAL HUMAN FLAW

From our very origins in Adam and Eve, Biblical faith understands that human beings are a fallen, imperfect species. In fact, since that couple fell to the Snake's deception, we're naturally self-centered, not wholly unlike animals. We're focused on self-preservation and not on each other, much less on God's larger purposes for us. Our human hard drive includes that flaw, which causes us *to miss the mark* God has set for us—the literal Hebrew meaning of *to sin*.

That flaw traps a husband and wife in its nearsighted vision, keeping each from seeing the other accurately—that is, with God's eyes.

What's more, our sin-nature keeps us from seeing God accurately, namely, as our Father. It not only compels us to scorn God's protective standards, but blinds us to His very presence—and thereby, to His power and victory amid our conflicts.

That's why the Father sent Jesus—to reveal Himself fully and empower us to do what He has said is best for us. "But for you who welcome (the Spirit of Christ), you in whom he dwells," Paul encourages,

> "—even though *you still experience all the limitations of sin*—you yourself experience life on God's terms.... God's Spirit touches our spirits and confirms who we really are. We know who he is, and we know who we are: *Father and children.* (Rom. 8:14-15TMB italics mine)

Certainly, most of us enter marriage with the hope of being loved. But the avenue to that simple goal is often misconstrued by our self-centered human sin-nature.

To the world, marriage is about having someone to love you. To Father God, it's about knowing the One who loves both of you, and Who empowers you thereby to love each other (see "Go to the Source for Love" in *Healing the Masculine Soul*).

It's surprisingly simple when you think about it. If the goal is for both of you to be loved, then let each of you focus on loving the other.

Done. You're both loved.

By definition, a Christian marriage grows in the character of Christ—who did not wait for us to love Him before He sacrificed Himself for us. Faithful husbands and wives, therefore, don't sit back and wait for the other to love you. That's a recipe for resentment.

Too often, our self-centered human nature leads us to charge each other, "You violated the terms of this relationship—that is, my terms. You're not giving me the love I need!"

That's not the voice of God's Spirit empowering you to mature love. Rather, it's a childish pity party, fueled by a crippling fear that you have no love to give—because you haven't trusted your true Father and received His love.

It's simple fact: You can't give what you don't have.

"How can I think about giving love to my husband/wife," that all-too-human voice complains, "when I need it so badly myself?"

It's simple faith: By going to the Source of love to get it.

God does not hold you accountable for whether your spouse loves you the way you want. But *He does hold you accountable for whether you love your spouse the way He loves you*. What's more, He has provided in Jesus all that you need to do that. In Holy Spirit, He's with you: ready, able, and indeed, eager to give you all the love you need to be the husband or wife He's called you to be.

Like most of us, at times my own immature expectations have caused me to miss God's mark in my marriage. As Paul explained to the Christians in Rome,

> Focusing on the self is the opposite of focusing on God. Anyone completely absorbed in self ignores God, ends up thinking more about self than God. That person ignores who God is and what he is doing. …. But if God himself has taken up residence in your life, you can hardly be thinking more of yourself than of him (Rom. 8:5-9TMB)

Without giving God "residence in your life," you soon discover that your own human power just isn't enough to overcome your natural impulse to focus on yourself. "I know that good does not live in me—

that is, in my human nature," as Paul confesses. "For even though the desire to do good is in me, I am not able to do it" (Rom. 7:18).

Every human being therefore bears an overwhelming—indeed, unbearable sense of shame for not measuring up to the man or woman God created you to be. Through the lens of that shame, it's easy to see God as an exacting taskmaster and judge who sets us up to fail and be punished.

I'M OK, YOU'RE NOT OK

Desperate to cover our shame and avoid such condemnation, we pretend righteousness by striving to appear better than others. "I'm OK, because you're not OK," we think. Thus, the Pharisee who thanked God he was "not a sinner…like everybody else" (Luke 18:11).

And thus, a husband and wife fight to prove "I'm right and you're wrong!"

This judgment and division often bind couples in conflict, as the legacy of shame-based religion. "It's just me and thee," as the old joke scoffs, "and I ain't so sure about thee." Translation, "The more shame I need to cover in myself, the more I need you to be wrong/bad so I can appear more right(eous) by comparison."

"Dear friends," John counters clearly and simply, "let us love one another, because love comes from God. Whoever loves is as child of God and knows God. Whoever does not love does not know God, for God is love" (1 John 4:7,8 italics mine).

This Father's love is not a zero-sum game; there's plenty to go around for everyone. His goal when couples argue is therefore *neither to lift up the one who is "right" nor to put down the one who is "wrong," but rather, to bless all who surrender to Him.* His love covers any shame and opens your hearts to His grace and healing.

Yes, God made husbands and wives different. "If both of you are the same," as another has noted, "one of you is unnecessary." But the difference does not mean that one is better than the other.

"Don't...read too much into the differences here between men and women," as Paul cautions. "Let's quit going through these 'who's first' routines" (1 Corinth. 11:11,12TMB).

Judging one gender as superior or inferior to the other, as sexism, is not simply cruel; it's an unholy distortion of God's image. It's eating from the Tree of the Knowledge of Good and Evil, separating men and women unto today from God and each other (see Mary's Chapter 4, "For Better, for Worse: Letting Go of Judgments").

That's why He told Adam and Eve to stay away from that tree and focus instead on the Tree of Life, that is, Jesus. Without surrendering to Jesus in our conflicts, therefore, we remain blinded by animal self-interest.

SEDUCED BY SHAME

When we see God clearly in Jesus, however, we see each other at last as His beloved son or daughter. That means *you can see others who call God "Father" as brothers and sisters—even your spouse— and thereby, worthy of the same love and grace you have received from Him* (see 2 Corinth. 1:1-5).

When we see Father God falsely, as merely judging and condemning, we're easily seduced by shame into hiding our sin and brokenness—like Adam and Eve, turning it over to the prince of Darkness to stir deeper division. Ultimately, we see each other falsely as well.

In particular, you don't want your spouse to see how imperfect you are, because you fear the shame of his/her judgment and condemnation. In quarrels, you want to hide your weakness for fear the other will take advantage and just hurt you more.

Jesus offers couples the way out of this vicious cycle.

On the cross, he was ultimately weak before the powers of this world. Significantly, however, *he did not surrender in his weakness to the world, but rather, to the Father* (see Luke 23:46). That's what allowed God's strength to manifest in and through Him against the enemy, even beyond death to life eternal in the resurrection.

Surrendering to the Father releases the power of God's Spirit in and through the followers of Jesus even today—even in your marriage. Resolving an argument is therefore not about surrendering to your spouse, but rather, surrendering to Jesus and allowing Him to draw you together by drawing you back to the Father.

Thus, the Apostle Paul prayed that the Christians at Ephesus "would know how very great is God's power at work in us who believe. This power is the same as the mighty strength which he used when he raised Christ from death and seated him at his right side in the heavenly world" (Ephes. 1:19).

This means that whatever has died in your marriage—from love and attraction to compassion and respect—the Spirit of God can restore. In fact, *you don't have to trust your spouse before talking over your differences; you just have to trust Jesus.*

"I don't always trust you," as Mary declared early in our marriage after a fight, "but I trust your relationship with the Father. I know you'll go to Him and He'll show you things from His perspective." In fact, she reassured me that she always prays He'll do that for me!

I confess, I don't always like what He shows me, and too often, I balk. Knowing Father God's love for you both, however, allows you to yield your "right to be right" and *enjoy the freedom to be real.*

In fact, you can even listen to your partner's side of the story (what a concept!). That's not weakness, but supreme courage and faith.

In her song, "Strong Enough to Bend," Tanya Tucker sings about a tree that's "never been broken by the wind" because "it's strong enough to bend." In the same sense, she says, a relationship "will last forever if we're strong enough to bend." In fact, "you can't take back" something hurtful you've said, but if you can say later, "Hey, well I could be wrong"—that humility assures "we can stand in the wind til the storm is gone."

This simple but powerful song portrays the freedom in saying, as another has put it, "I'm not OK and you're not OK—but that's OK." There's the true confession which the Father honors. It's true because He accepts you both in your fallen nature. What's more, He's sent Jesus as The Way back to Himself, in order to make both husband and wife OK in His sight—and thereby, *able to talk together without shaming each other* (see John 14:6).

Surrendered to Him, that is, we don't need to hide our shame by putting each other down, simply because our shame is gone. "There is therefore now no condemnation for those who are in Christ Jesus," as Paul declares (Rom. 8:1), echoing the Psalmist: "Those who look to the Lord are radiant; their faces are never covered with shame" (Ps. 34:5NIV).

That trust in Jesus' saving work rescues a fighting couple from the awful pit of division and destruction.

ANIMAL FIGHT-OR-FLIGHT

Our self-centered human nature, meanwhile, leads a couple to hide from God and thereby, from each other. Thus, after The Fall, Adam and Eve not only ducked behind the bushes but covered themselves with fig leaves. When you turn away from God, that is, your self-centeredness takes over; when you don't like what your spouse has done, your animal fight-or-flight response kicks in and you want either to lash out in vengeance or to shut down and run away (see Gen. 3:8-10).

That's great for couples who love to fight. But those who fight to love know that the victory comes when you turn toward God together and, in the covering of His grace, *look honestly at your own part in the quarrel.*

Shame makes you want to hide your fault when you're fighting. Jesus, however, enables us freely to confess and expose your sin so God can overcome its effects—even as a bandage must eventually come off for healing. Couples who don't trust Him to enter their conflicts learn a tough lesson: covering your wrongdoing only hands it over to the prince of Darkness to fester and cause further division and distance.

When you're sick, that is, you seek a doctor to diagnose your problem, so you can get healed. Similarly, you want to know when you miss God's mark so you can go to the Great Physician and tell Him where it hurts—that is, where you need healing. "Investigate my life, O God," as the warrior King David wrote:

> Find out everything about me. Cross-examine and test me, get a clear picture of what I'm about; see for yourself whether I've done anything wrong—then guide me on the road to eternal life. (Ps. 139:23.24TMB).

This determination to expose your hidden faults so God can heal you, is a Kingdom warrior's credo. That's fighting to love.

In fact, couples who pray so boldly, like King David, know they have a convenient, trustworthy "cross-examiner" at hand in their very home.

No one, that is, knows your imperfection as intimately as your spouse, because no one suffers its effects more painfully. The question is, Will he/she uncover my faults with grace, or with judgment?

At times, marriage differences can stir decidedly unloving feelings; two creatures with an inborn impulse to turn away from God are sure to rub each other the wrong way sooner or later and create sparks. In that sense, marriage is a holy diagnostic tool which highlights your imperfection—and thereby *enables humble couples to identify their brokenness and seek God's healing together.*

Husbands and wives surrendered to The Great Physician, that is, are eminently qualified and divinely equipped to reveal each other's brokenness: "Honey, what do you see in me that hurts you and makes it hard for us to connect?" you can ask your spouse.

To whatever extent that question stirs fear instead of hope in you as a husband or wife, you love to fight. You simply haven't trusted Jesus enough for Him to heal you.

After all, from His Kingdom perspective, your sin-nature separates you from the Almighty Father. It's a chink in your armor that allows the enemy to bypass His protection.

Seasoned warriors don't want to go into battle with defective shields. Thus, a magazine interviewer once asked radio personality Garrison Keillor what freedom meant to him as a Christian? "Not to be afraid that my lies will be discovered," Keillor replied wisely.[7]

How simple that sounds—and yet, as most married couples will readily testify, it's not easy. Rather than unite together against the common enemy of division and contention, too often it's easy to hide your fault by casting your spouse as the enemy, and open fire.

COMMON ENEMY

This fundamental, even natural deception beckons the father of Lies and often fuels conflict in marriages even as in the larger world. "For we are not fighting against human beings," as Paul noted, "but against the wicked spiritual forces in the heavenly world" (Ephes. 6:12).

What, indeed, if your spouse is not the enemy? What if a larger-than-human power conspires to divide and destroy your marriage by baiting you both into quarrels? What if that enemy has been decisively defeated and his work overcome by Jesus?

Indeed, what if "the Spirit who is in you is more powerful than the spirit in those who belong to the world"? (1 John 4:4).

If that doesn't stir hope, you're tuned in to the enemy and not to your Father.

In any case, gaining His larger perspective of *fighting together against a common enemy* is basic to a trusting, intimate Christian marriage.

Sure, it's awfully hard if not impossible to see that reality through the eyes of our self-centered sin-nature. But that's why Jesus came: to free us from our near-sighted natural vision in order to show us each other with God's eyes.

"Father, show me my spouse the way You see him/her" is therefore the breakthrough question amid conflict.

Dan, married for 21 years and "tired of all the fighting at home" came to me furious at his wife for "criticizing me all the time." (Throughout the book, names in all case histories are not real).

"Let's pray about it," I suggested eventually. "Go ahead and tell Jesus how frustrating her criticism is, and ask Him to show you her the way He sees her."

"Jesus, I'm just so fed up with all her putting me down and criticizing me!" Dan burst out immediately. "Show me how you see her." He fell silent for a moment, then sat up in surprise.

"That's weird!" he declared. "This picture of her came into my mind, like a little girl, kind of scared and curled up in a corner."

"If that's the way Jesus sees her, ask Him to come into that picture," I offered, "and give him permission to show you whatever He wants to do about it."

"OK," Dan nodded. Praying quietly, soon he shook his head in amazement. "Jesus goes over and just holds her in his arms. When he does, she starts to cry."

"What does that tell you about your wife?" I asked.

Dan sat quietly for a minute, a mixture of confusion and concern. "I guess…," he offered finally, "she's really hurting."

ANGER HIDES PAIN

"I can understand how she's made you angry," I offered, "but Jesus seems to be showing you that her criticism is really a cover-up for some deep pain that she's afraid to face—or to let you see."

Knitting his brow, Dan thought it over and sighed deeply.

I smiled. "I think that with His hug, Jesus is showing you what He wants to do about that pain," I offered. "Now who do you suppose He could get to do that for Him?"

Nodding, Dan smiled back. "OK, I get it," he said at last. "I'll do that."

I reached out with a fist bump. "Good move, brother!" I exclaimed. "Your Father will honor you for loving His daughter like that.

"And you know what?" I added, "so will she."

We then asked Holy Spirit to show us any enemy spirits which had bound up his wife. Several came to mind, including abuse, isolation, and timidity—and in the name of Jesus, he cast them out of her. He then prayed for the blood of Jesus to cleanse her from all effects of those spirits and for the Father's blessing to replace those works of the enemy with the work of His Holy Spirit, in compassion, fellowship, and courage (see 2 Tim. 1:7).

When Dan and I met a week later, he told me he asked his wife if she would sit together with him on the couch without saying anything, so they could just hold each other. "It took a few minutes—she got tensed up—and I wasn't sure if I'd done the right thing or not. But I just held onto her and kept saying 'Jesus, Jesus, Jesus' in my mind. After a bit I could feel her relaxing some, and it was good.

"I'm not sure how all that works," Dan confessed, "but I can only say we haven't had a fight in a week. That's a record for us!"

Seeing God's heart for your loved one stirs compassion, which enables a husband and wife to forgive and bless each other. Best of all, it allows the Father of you both to enter the conflict, so you can stop the wounding and instead fight together for each other's healing.

Here lies Good News for couples: the Resurrected Christ has left us His very Spirit to fill us. By His Spirit's power, you can receive the Father's compassionate heart and see His transforming vision for your spouse, as He did for Dan.

Granted, when the wounds are festering and accusations are flying between the two of you, it's hard to step back—much less above it all—and see each other as God sees. In fact, you're easily duped into defending yourself by lashing back and thereby, doing the enemy's work of judgment and destruction rather than Father God's work of blessing and healing.

That's why you need Holy Spirit to keep you focused on Him.

When a husband and wife are at odds, therefore, you're up against the self-centered sin-nature in each of you, which compels you to focus entirely on yourself and proudly turn away from God and your spouse. Overcoming this requires humble confession of sin before God and each other, and seeking Holy Spirit's wisdom and power to heal you of its effects in both of you.

In addition, our spiritual enemy can take advantage of your disunity and sabotage God's work in your marriage (see *A Couples' Guide to Spiritual Warfare*).

What's most important to realize for now, is that the Father of you both is in control, even of these powers both within you and outside you that would set the two of you against each other. He's on your side together. He wants to heal your marriage.

To demonstrate that decisively, He sent Jesus to overcome your sin nature with His overwhelming grace and "to destroy the works of the devil" (1 John 3:8).

GOD'S LARGER PERSPECTIVE

This larger perspective and its victorious power is what makes Christian marriages different from others. The fact that we divorce as often as non-believers means that Christian husbands and wives are not owning up to our sins against each other, seeking healing for our wounds, and counter-attacking any attending enemy spirits.

Think of it this way: When a husband and wife fight, God's male-and-female image is split—and they don't reflect the whole nature of God.

The Father therefore wants couples to be united for His own sake, so He can be seen for who He is. He's not out to condemn your sin of pulling away from Him and hurting each other; rather, He wants to overcome it by throwing the weight of His power toward restoring you back together.

When you fight together for your marriage, therefore, it's good to remember that God is on your side, and mediates His saving power the more as you both want to be on His side. Dare to stay connected to your Father amid the struggle, by crying out for and submitting to Him. Trust His readiness to honor your faith and His power to bring you both back together, even closer than before.

I'm not saying just to shut up, give in to whatever your spouse says, and stuff your feelings. Such compression is a recipe for explosion, designed by the prince of Darkness.

Nor am I telling you to raise the volume and unleash counter-accusations against your spouse, no matter how "truthful."

I'm urging the two of you *humbly to seek a third opinion together.*

In fact, I'm talking about the Father of you both, who's been waiting for you to ask Him.

I'll show you now what that can look like.

Early the next morning, Elisha's servant got up, went out of the house, and saw the Syrian troops with their horses and chariots surrounding the town. He went back to Elisha and declared, "We are doomed, Sir! What shall we do?"

"Don't be afraid," Elisha answered. "We have more on our side than they have on theirs." Then he prayed, "O Lord, open his eyes and let him see!" The Lord answered his prayer, and Elisha's servant looked up and saw the hillside covered with horses and chariots of fire all around Elisha. (2 Kings 6:15-17)

Father, I pray for any couples reading this who may feel afraid and discouraged: Open their eyes to focus not on the enemy's threat but on Your promise. Please, reveal your presence and power to them.

> When couples fight, the key question is not, Who's right?, but rather, What's God trying to teach us?

3

Never Waste a Good Fight

Getting a Third Opinion from the Great Physician

God is our shelter and strength, always ready to help in times of trouble.... The Lord Almighty is with us; the God of Jacob is our refuge. He stops wars all over the world; he breaks bows, destroys spears, and sets shields on fire.

"Stop fighting!" he says, "and know that I am God, *supreme among the nations, supreme over the world."* Psalm 46:1,7,9-10, (italics mine)

"DO YOU AND MARY ever fight together?"

The conference Question and Answer session had been routine until this unexpected response. A hint of shame beckoned, and I balked—and then a perfect face-saving answer occurred to me.

"Mary and I fight together all the time," I replied, smiling. As the group of men stirred with surprise, I added, "We fight together side by side, against the enemy who wants to divide us!"

The men sat uncertain, and in that moment of grace, I knew I needed to be real. "Actually," I allowed, "it's not always that way—and even when it is, it's not as easy as it sounds. But that's what we aim for."

In fact, growing relationships often require "airing disagreements," if only so the prince of Darkness doesn't leverage hidden wounds. "If you become angry," as Paul exhorted, "do not let your anger lead you into sin, and do not stay angry all day. Don't give the Devil a chance" (Ephes. 4:36,37).

The Father is not surprised or worried when a husband and wife disagree and even get angry at each other. He just doesn't want you to sin by turning away from Him and thereby giving the powers of evil freedom to hurt you.

Before you get into an argument together, therefore—preferably when you're both in an agreeable mode—I urge you: agree on the basic goal of all such "discussions."

"When couples fight," as my seminary pastor Rev. Herb Davis said years ago, "they always think the question is, Who's right? But that's not the question, because it's too easy to answer. Just ask either one and they'll both tell you, '*I'm* right.' Otherwise, they wouldn't be fighting.

"The real question for couples who want to grow together is, What's God trying to teach us?"

SELF-CENTERED AGENDAS

This simple illustration portrays the primary "fruit" of the "Tree of the Knowledge of Good and Evil" (Gen. 2:9-17). If we translate this as the "Tree of the Knowledge of What's Right and What's Wrong," when tempers flare it easily becomes the Tree of the Knowledge of *Who's* Right and *Who's* Wrong." That's why Father God warned the very first man and woman not to eat that fruit, since doing so destroys trust, stirs judgment, and leads to the death of relationship.

From this perspective, you can see the Tree of Life in contrast, as the living presence of Jesus. The fruit of this Tree is the grace of the Father, which allows you to trust His love, forget who's right or wrong, and learn what He wants to teach you.

When "opponents" can get beyond their self-centered agendas, that is, they're ready together to confess and surrender their sin-nature to God. That's when He can begin not only to heal them of wounds that caused the argument, but teach them to avoid future ones.

The Apostle Paul knew this. When a dispute arose among the church at Corinth, he urged the dissident parties to look beyond their squabbles and focus instead on what God was doing to strengthen His Church:

> The focus of my letter *wasn't on punishing the offender, but on getting you to take responsibility for the health of the church.* So if you forgive him, I forgive him. Don't think I'm carrying around a list of personal grudges. The fact is that I'm joining in with your forgiveness, as Christ is with us, guiding us. After all, *we don't want to unwittingly give Satan an opening for yet more mischief*—we're not oblivious to his sly ways! (2 Corinth. 2:9-11TMB, italics mine)

Similarly, couples who together seek "the health" of their marriage—and not simply to identify and "punish the offender"—open themselves to Holy Spirit's grace and guidance. They don't want to "carry around a list of personal grudges" or accommodate such destructive "mischief" from the enemy. Instead, they renounce the natural urge for vengeance, ask forgiveness of each other, and determine to fight together side by side in the Father's *super*-natural victory. In that process, they can spot the enemy's schemes and how to fight back successfully.

"Never waste a good conflict," as Christian authors David and Vera Mace put it in *How to Have a Happy Marriage*. "Our culture has deceived us by suggesting that marriage can be free from conflicts. On the contrary, conflict is an inevitable and integral part of a strong marriage."[8]

Sure, it's hard. But then, what's truly valuable rarely comes easily.

BLESSED FIGHT

Mary and I learned to value such a blessed fight during our first year of marriage.

Who can forget that season? For any first-year couples reading this book, we'll pause here for a moment of silence. I can only say that it gets better—a lot better, in fact, if you're willing to welcome Jesus into your struggles.

Maybe your own first year together was all honeymoon laughter-and-love 24/7. If so, I'm happy for you. I can only say that ours included considerable "adjustment."

Remember, the Father's goal is to demonstrate His overcoming power to you both. He has a purpose for your marriage, and in order to fulfill it you need to work as a team against a common enemy—as Paul describes the early church above (see Ephes. 2:8-10, 6:10ff). He wants to teach you how to do that, *and uses your own conflicts as lessons.*

Thus, lion cubs wrestle together, even growl and snarl, to prepare for their adult calling to hunt and fight later in the jungle. Like domestic kittens, their backs arch high, fur stands up, fangs show, and claws bare, as two pretend enemies launch themselves at each other amid hissing and howls.

Significantly, however, the two animals know when to stop short of harming each other; when the tussle gets too fierce, they leap apart. God has apparently ingrained that holy boundary in them as an instinctive awareness that destroying each other would defeat the larger purpose for their lives.

After all, they're not really enemies. They're brother and sister.

Husbands and wives, take note—and listen, please, to my story:

One evening in our newlywed season, Mary and I got into it over something. I don't even remember what set us off; I only know that it seemed awfully important at the time.

After trading shots for awhile, however, it was clear we'd gone down a rabbit hole, never to return unless some power greater than the two of us entered the fray. Yes, we're each highly educated, but sometimes that only means our barbs become more proficiently crafted.

Frustrated and scared—*how in the world were we going to get out of this dark place together?*—I sighed deeply, un-grit my teeth, and girded my loins.

"This argument is over," I declared, taking Mary's hand.

In previous generations, this announcement commonly meant that both partners stopped talking and went their separate ways. Of course, because everyone was now quiet, peace was restored to the village and everyone lived happily ever after.

Not.

They don't call the devil "the prince of Darkness" for nothing. In his "sly ways," as Paul cautioned, he thrills to see couples shut up and seethe quietly.

So I pressed ahead. "I'm tired of hurting each other," I sighed, shaking my head in dismay. "Come on, let's pray."

Wounded, angry, and confused, I reached out my hand to Mary. Thankfully, she took it—with similar dismay—and I drew her with me into our bedroom. There, we knelt down together at the foot of our bed.

Forgive me if this seems elementary or simplistic. If the two of you do this all the time, give me some grace. I just couldn't think of anything else to do.

This kneel-and-pray-together approach to "conflict resolution" was not in my hard drive. I'd never done it before that day. In fact, I'd never read about it, seen or heard it done or taught anywhere—not at home growing up, not between other married friends, not in any movie, not in my seminary curriculum, nor even in any of the many churches I attended growing up and since.

Today, since our wedding in 1990, I haven't seen anything better.

It's simple, but not easy.

FOUR HOLES IN THE CARPET

Indeed, this wasn't the only time Mary and I knelt together. In that first year, we wore four holes in the bedroom carpet.

Speaking of simple, it's worth noting here that the word "kneel" comes from the root word for "knee." That's the joint between your ankle and your hip. When it bends you get smaller—and that's the idea.

In any case, as the two of us knelt side by side, I took another measured breath and led the way. "O God," I cried out, modeling after

King David in Psalm 139:23,24, "search my wife's heart, and find out what wickedness there is within her!" (Freely translated from THB— *The Husband's Bible*).

OK, actually I didn't say that—though I confess the thought did cross my mind. Instead, with a nod to David's asking God to "search *my* heart" for evil, I struggled to give it my best shot.

"Father!" I sighed out loud, still holding Mary's hand tightly, in order not to turn and run. "We give up. To you. We've done our best and we just keep hurting each other more. We can't seem to stop it. Please, speak to us, Father! If there's something I'm doing as a man that's keeping us fighting each other like this, please show me."

After a moment of silence, to my wonder and awe, I then heard the voice of a marvelous wife kneeling beside me say, "Yes, Father—if there's something I'm doing as a woman that's making us fight, please show me."

Astonished, I turned and looked at her, my jaw agape.

Even with such amazing grace about us, however, I confess I turned back and knelt there fuming. *OK, Father!* I prayed quietly. *Now's the time—she's open. Go ahead and speak. Mary hears from you. You're the same yesterday, today, and tomorrow. You were there—you know she's wrong and it happened like I say. Just tell her the truth!*

Hopefully, I waited—but heard nothing either from the Father or from Mary.

LISTEN TO HER

And then suddenly, three simple words popped into my mind: "Listen to her."

"Listen to her," Father? I echoed in silent frustration. *What do you mean? I've been listening to her for half an hour! You're all-knowing. You know it didn't happen like she says. Please, just make* her *listen to* me!

Frustrated, I waited but heard nothing more. During the fight, I'd already exhausted all my intelligent, insightful—and not a few unseemly options; I could only press on in my prayer and try another avenue.

Father, you know I love your Word, I prayed righteously under my breath. *Please, give me a Scripture to get us out of this mess!*

The Word I did not love, however, returned: "Listen to her."

Struggling, I tried again. *Please, Father—how about a* rhema *word of knowledge? Yes, come Holy Spirit!*

"Listen to her," I heard yet again.

Exasperated, I cut to the chase. *Father, look: You know I'm right— just tell her!*

Suddenly, it struck me: He never said I was wrong. He just said, "Listen to her."

As I knelt there puzzled and frustrated, suddenly my beloved's voice cut in from beside me. "I'm not getting anything from the Lord," Mary said, turning to me and shrugging her shoulders in confusion, "—are you?"

I drew up. "Well…," I offered hesitantly—humble Christian that I am—"I… I don't really know if it's from the Lord or not. I mean, you know, it could be just me."

(After all, the Bible says we see only as "in a mirror dimly" in this present age—right? You can read it yourself in First Corinthians 13:12.)

"OK…," Mary offered, genuinely at a loss, "but if you've got anything at all, let's try it anyhow and see."

"Well, I don't think it's really all that…I mean…"

Pausing uneasily, I realized the only way out of this was through it. Apparently the dim mirror was about to become more clear—and uncomfortable. *Come on, Father,* I prayed quietly, *walk me through this!*

"OK...," I began hesitantly, gathering my courage, "the gist was kind of like..., maybe...I haven't been listening to you very well...."

That got Mary's attention. Straightening up, she looked me square in the eye, focused and intense.

"Maybe...," I allowed again, meeting her gaze and pushing through, "I mean, if you could just...tell me once more what you were saying, I'll try my best to listen."

A tentative squint of Mary's eyes said, *Do I dare trust this dude one more time?* After a significant pause, however, with measured breath—and not just a little faith—she began talking to me about her being afraid, including something painful that had happened to her before we ever met.

No wonder she was so upset! I thought.

Minutes later, we were in each other's arms, asking forgiveness for hurting each other.

I could almost hear the Father huff in disgust, "And you wanted to be right!"

RIGHT OR REAL?

When we were holding each other, I thanked Mary for being so real and for asking God to show her how she shared in the disagreement.

"Well," she offered matter-of-factly, "you led the way."

Let me tell you, folks: as a husband, it doesn't get much better than that.

Still, it's not that I was so noble in my intentions, courageous in my faith, or eloquent in my prayers. I was just desperate in my need—and trusted that *desperation is solid currency in the Kingdom of God.*

By the grace of God, I did it right. That day, however, I learned a simple but powerful lesson: There's something better than doing it right. It's being real—before God and the one you love, trusting Him to draw you back together.

The Psalmist proclaims that in this chapter's opening scripture.

To see each other with God's eyes is first and foremost to know that both of you are His children. No father wants to see his children fighting and hurting each other. Rather, this ancient song declares how Father God determines to stop human battles: not as the world, by lifting up one side and humbling the other, but rather, *by lifting up Himself and humbling you both.*

In this Good News Bible translation, the well-known verse "Be still and know that I am God" is correctly translated not as a sanitized, milquetoast invitation to meditate quietly, as so often mis-applied. Rather, it's a furious Father's commanding His children to drop their weapons against each other—to "***STOP FIGHTING!***," submit together to His lordship, and focus their energies instead on what He's doing to unite them.

Unto today, I believe it's the ultimate solution to arguments, whether between couples, church members, or nations.

During another argument that first year, Mary and I went to the Father yet again and prayed for Him to come and reconcile us. When I asked Him to show me anything I had done or said that was getting in His way, I heard no words. Eventually, however, an old memory came to mind from high school, when I drove to pick up my date at her house and her father answered the door.

"Where are you going tonight with my daughter?" this man much larger than me had demanded.

Intimidated, nevertheless I accounted for myself. "To the sock hop at the gym," I replied—hastily adding, "Sir!"

"When are you bringing her home?" he barked.

"Well—Sir—the dance is over at ten and I thought…"

"Ten fifteen!" the father commanded.

RESPECT GOD'S DAUGHTER

And indeed, that night I danced a bit faster than every rock 'n roll beat and overlooked Big Boy Burgers and even a few stop signs on the way home. Quicker than you can say "life insurance," I had that young lady back in her driveway—and straightaway to the front door.

Meanwhile, back in our bedroom, I knelt puzzled. *What's this memory about, Father?* I asked quietly in prayer.

And then, I knew: even as the father of my date had made it clear I was to respect his daughter, Father God was telling me the same thing about His daughter Mary:

"How you treat Mary, you answer to me!"

Suddenly a new sense of respect arose in me for my wife. With that, I turned and asked her to forgive me for some unkind things I'd said, and promised I'd try to be more understanding. She followed suit and asked me to forgive her also. Once again, we were chagrined at our childishness—and awed at our Father's grace.

A note here about making up: Just saying "I'm sorry" may make you feel like you've done the right thing, but it doesn't finish the job. It's a good start, but that statement alone won't open the door to your partner's heart, because the subject is "I." It's all about you.

"*I'm* sorry" falls short because it maintains your defenses and prompts no response or input from the other. It could easily mean, "I'm sorry you were hurt"—that is, "I didn't really do anything wrong, but it's too bad you're so thin-skinned that it bothered you. In any case, I'm being humble, so I deserve the kudos."

If you're really sorry for what you did, then you wish you hadn't done it because you see how it hurt your beloved. So demonstrate your contrition by *noting specifically* what you did that hurt him/her, for example, "Please forgive me for saying that unkind thing/not letting you speak/walking out on the conversation/yelling at you/…?"

Making your spouse the subject and not you requires more faith—but that's the point: It allows the other person freedom to respond. Sure, it's risky; asking forgiveness means keeping your heart open to trust someone, even when he/she might likely want to pay you back.

In fact, it's not natural. Again, that's the point. Risky vulnerability like that is *super*natural—like Jesus on the cross. Only the faithful can fight to love like that.

In fact, the very risk itself draws both partners into the reconciliation process, challenging each to demonstrate a deeper love—and faith in its Source. Asking forgiveness is better than saying "I'm sorry," because it gives Father God more room to work in and through each of you, even to use the conflict to draw you closer.

Often when the two of you cry out to Jesus and press ahead into the battle like this, His saving hand will leave you both with a rush of thanksgiving and praise. What's more, it can stir a readiness to celebrate the victory physically.

A high five is definitely in order. But let's not forget to enjoy every blessing: making love can often be best after a fight clears the air. I figure it's the Father's reward to you both for a job well done. A good fight, when hidden pains and fears are finally expressed to each other and prayed over, releases inhibitions and demonstrates that what you feared most in expressing yourself didn't really have the destructive power you thought it had.

Maybe it got messy. But you took a fearful step of faith and trusted God and each other, and that opened a new door for Him to straighten you both out.

When the tension is gone at last, there's definitely something freeing about coming through the fight together, asking each other's forgiveness, and pledging to act differently next time. A joyful "We did it!" can do wonders for intimacy.

Here, I would humbly suggest a motel getaway, minimum four stars, in-room Jacuzzi preferred.

DAREDEVIL HUMILITY

It's helpful to remember that, regardless of who's most vocal, wounding by both parties lies at the root of most marital arguments. Still, in order to spur the Father's perspective, one partner needs the courage to lead the way—that is, freely and humbly to confess his/her own role in the conflict first, without expecting the other to do so.

That's literally dare-devil humility. As such, it defines leadership in the Kingdom of God.

After all, Jesus did not say, "When you confess your sin and clean up your act, I'll go to the cross for you." Indeed, "it was while we were yet sinners Christ died for us" (Rom. 5:8). That's bold faith: laying your heart open, calling on the Father, and trusting Him for the outcome.

At the end of the day, that is, you're not accountable for how your spouse treated you. Like the arresting memory of my high school date's father, however, you will answer for how you treated your spouse.

Let's face it: no matter how "mature" we may think we are, sometimes we squabble like third graders. It's helpful then to remember this hallowed principle of mature faith: "Last one to the cross is a rotten egg."

Sure, sometimes it seems like there's no way to get out of this vicious cycle still loving each other. In fact, that's true if you only see things from your own, natural view.

But Jesus has broken through our natural fears and blazed the trail ahead.

Be bold and follow Him.

My Christian brothers and sisters, please: don't let that fight between Mary and me be wasted. Remember: A bad fight turns good *not when one party surrenders to the other, but when both surrender together to God.*

Give Him a chance to prove it.

> The essence of Original Sin is presuming to judge as God judges. Jesus came so a husband and wife can let God be the Judge—and thereby, free you both to love each other.

4

For Better or Worse

Letting Go of Judgments

by **Mary Dalbey**, Ph.D.

So where does that leave you when you criticize a brother? And where does that leave you when you condescend to a sister? I'd say it leaves you looking pretty silly—or worse. Eventually, we're all going to end up kneeling side by side in the place of judgment, facing God. Rom. 14:10 TMB

REMEMBER THESE WEDDING vows?

I, (name), take you (name), to be my lawfully wedded (wife/husband), to have and to hold from this day forward, for better or for worse, for richer for poorer, in sickness and

in health, to love and to cherish from this day
forward, as long as we both shall live.

"For better or for worse"—for the rest of your life!

What were you thinking?!!

What was the worst thing you could imagine back then—his leaving dirty socks on the floor? Her wearing curlers to bed?

You probably thought the *better* was going to overshadow the *worse* every day of your life together—right?

So what happened? When did the honeymoon end? Where did Paradise go?

Actually, the same thing that happened in Paradise to Adam and Eve has likely happened in your marriage. That's right.

In the beginning, the man and woman were made not only *for* each other, but literally *from* each other. So Eve was made out of Adam's own rib to be his "suitable companion" (Gen. 2:18):

> Then the Lord God made a woman from
> the rib, and he brought her to the man. "At
> last!" the man exclaimed. "This one is bone
> from my bone, and flesh from my flesh! She
> will be called 'woman,' because she was taken
> from 'man'." This explains why a man leaves
> his father and mother and is joined to his wife,
> and the two are united into one. Now the man
> and his wife were both naked, but they felt no
> shame. (Gen. 2:22-25 NLT)

Adam and Eve were perfectly innocent before God, and therefore could be perfectly intimate with each other: "naked, but they felt no shame" in their sexuality, in their vulnerability, in their communication. And yet later that very day, only eight verses afterward, we read, "That evening they heard the Lord God walking in the garden, and they hid from him among the trees" (Gen. 3:8).

How did everything go so wrong, so fast?

FORBIDDEN TREE

The Enemy lied to them and they bought it—plain and simple.

God had warned Adam and Eve that they would die if they ate from the Tree of the Knowledge of Good and Evil. But the snake deceived them into thinking that God was holding back from them something wonderfully good in that tree.

"That's not true; you will not die," the snake told Eve. "God said that because he knows that when you eat it you will be like God and know what is good and what is evil" (Gen. 3:4,5NIV).

At Creation in Eden, Adam and Eve thereby defined the essence of Original Sin as *presuming to judge as God judges.*

In his book, *Repenting of Religion*[9], Greg Boyd explains that in eating from the forbidden tree, they stole the knowledge of good and evil and were seduced into taking God's place by judging others. The problem here is simply that we're not God; our sin-nature, in fact, causes us to judge not with God's eyes, but rather, from our own narrow, self-centered view.

Adam and Eve started out with pure love for God and for each other. Then quickly, they went to hiding from each other behind their fig leaves and from God in the bushes. All too often, that's what happens to marriages today—even yours. After the honeymoon bliss, our differences sooner or later get categorized as "good" or "bad/evil" and spark arguments. We then pull away from each other, hide from God, try to muddle through it without Him, and end up further apart.

Even now, most couples know from frustrating experience that you can be loving each other one minute and fighting the next. *With the capacity to judge, it's not far from Paradise to a fight.*

How does that happen?

Remember, the snake seduced Eve by assassinating God's character, casting Him as an egotistic taskmaster who forbids certain behavior just because He doesn't want us to know as much as He knows.

In fact, God is a good Father who wants what's best for His children. His boundaries, therefore, are not just harsh commandments, but rather, protective warnings—even promises of fulfillment. "Please, my beloved children," He's begging, "do what I tell you so you can stay safe and fulfill my plans for your life."

BOUNDARIES FOR PROTECTION

Good parents, that is, set boundaries in order to protect their children from danger, so they can grow up to lead fulfilling lives. Similary, when we heed the Father's warning and respect His boundaries, safety and "long life" follow (Deut. 11:21).

When Adam and Eve don't listen to the Father's warnings, however, severe consequences sabotage their relationship:

> Then he said to the woman, "I will sharpen the pain of your pregnancy, and in pain you will give birth. And you will desire to control your husband, but he will rule over you" … And he said to the man, … "Because of what you have done, … you will have to work hard all your life to make the ground produce enough food for you." (Genesis 3:16 NLT; :18TEV).

So much for the honeymoon!

When they distrust God and reject His boundaries, the man and woman choose no longer to be defined in relationship with the Father, as beloved son and daughter. Rather, when they leave the security of the Father's heart for them, they forget Whose they are, lose themselves in the world, and become subject to its false definitions: the woman now gets her identity from the man; the man now gets his identity from his work.

So much for God!

Literally since the beginning of time, this curse on the man and the woman lives on (see "Making a Living, or Making a Life: The Man and the Job" in Gordon's *Sons of the Father*). Even today, some Christians misinterpret the woman's punishment to mean that God intends the man to rule over the woman—when in fact, *that domineering relationship is the curse of sin, not the blessing of walking with God.*

Satan knew that eating from that tree would destroy Adam and Eve's trusting relationship with God, and thereby, with each other as well. In particular, the readiness to judge would short-circuit their intimacy. And so, "the knowledge of good and evil" invaded their hearts with suspicion, distrust, separation, and at last, judgment. Ultimately, it would lead to death—not only of their innocence, but literally, back "to the soil from which you came" (see Gen. 2:16,17; 3:19).

Here's how that works.

SHAME DESTROYS INTIMACY

In labeling "what is good and what is evil," sooner or later we evaluate and judge one another. That presumption breeds shame, which drives us apart. So in their shame, Adam and Eve covered their nakedness, and in that sense hid from each other, even as from God. Like us even today, they retreated from their true identity in the Father, no longer focusing on His love, but instead, on objective behavior standards—that is, on "what is good and what is evil."

Such legalism kills loving relationship—which thrives not on judging, but rather, on trusting. When they both covered themselves, they lost the freedom of innocent love and hid from God and each other. Any remaining shred of intimacy and mutual respect was lost when Adam threw Eve under the bus by blaming her for his fall: "The woman you put here with me gave me the fruit" (Gen. 3:12).

Like our spiritual ancestors in Paradise, we husbands and wives even today lose intimacy and pull apart when we judge what's good and what's bad in each other. We thereby presume to be in control "like God," as the Snake tempted (Gen. 3:4).

The lie is exposed when sooner or later, you find out you're not in control, that neither of you can define the other—or indeed, dictate the outcome of an argument. In fact, by trying to seize control from Father God, you're left trapped in your human sin-nature and its inadequate natural power. You've taken *super*natural control away from God and thereby left it to the enemy—who's happy to steal your love and drive you both further apart.

Ever since Adam and Eve fell to that temptation, we fancy that if we have the right knowledge, the right principles, and the right judgment, we can be like God. We not only fancy that we can control ourselves, but others as well. In the worst case, Christian spouses can do this with "Bible bullets," using scripture verses to justify themselves and lash back at each other.

Let's face it: the desire to control another person is often simply an attempt to protect yourself from pain.

And guess what? It works—because it's a sure-fire way to put distance between the two of you. In your isolation, you won't be hurt. But here's the catch: you won't be loved, either.

Sure, it's important to know when you feel discounted and hurt, and to ask God for wisdom how to talk about it together. But when you label what your spouse is doing as right or wrong, you've bitten the enemy's bait.

It's one thing to say, "I feel hurt." That requires being vulnerable and takes not just courage, but the self-respect that says "My feelings count." Being so real like that is risky; you can't control how the other responds. What's more, it's an act of faith, which opens the door not just to your heart, but for Father God to enter the conflict.

It's quite another thing to say, "What you did was wrong." That betrays a lack of self-respect by hiding behind judgment as a weapon. It says "My feelings don't carry any authority, so I need to strike back against you with shame."

It says the law has more power than our relationship. It's an act of defense which closes the door to your heart—and thereby, to Father God's Spirit.

Sure, being vulnerable is risky. There's no guarantee the other person will honor your feelings and listen. But it puts the ball in Father God's court to make His move—which increases His respect for you and the chances of His deeper healing.

When you judge the other person, you turn away from the Tree of Life. In fact, you distrust God, stop the flow of His Spirit, and attempt, rather, *to control the other person—which sets a wall between you.*

That's why Father God doesn't want His children to eat from the Tree of the Knowledge of Good and Evil—not, as the Snake charged, because He's an egomaniac, but because He wants His healing Spirit to flow freely between a husband and wife.

Yet that distrust in God endures unto today as the devil's pitchfork, spurring many a couple to hurl judgment at each other instead of inviting the Father's Spirit to teach them respect and compassion.

And so the "knowledge of good and evil" prompts a vicious, ping-pong cycle of judgment and defensive counter-judgment:

> "Why do you throw your dirty clothes on the floor right next to the hamper? You're such a slob!"

> Or,

> "Oh yeah? Well, how many times do I have to tell you not to spend so much money? You're so wasteful."

THE TREE OF LIFE

The Good News, meanwhile, is that there's another Tree in the Garden, through which Father God frees us from our lust for control. The Tree of Life, in fact, bears not the deadly fruit of distrust, judgment, and separation, but rather, "life abundant" in trust, grace, and intimacy (John 10:10).

The Tree of Life is not the Law, but Jesus Christ—who *fulfills* the Law by bearing its judgment Himself on the cross, *so we don't have to judge each other*. Instead, His sacrifice covers your sin and releases God's Spirit in you to love freely again, without judgment and shame, as in the Beginning (see Matt. 5:17). Unto today, the freedom Jesus brings to a marriage is *the same as the freedom Adam and Eve enjoyed together in Paradise before the snake stole it.*

In fact, "God loved the world so much that He gave His Only Son, so that everyone who believes in Him may not die but have eternal life." What's more, the very next verse declares that "God didn't go to all the trouble of sending His Son merely to point an accusing finger, telling the world how bad it was. He came to help, to put the world right again" (John 3:16 TEV, 17TMB).

Husbands and wives, please listen: if you want Jesus to restore freedom and intimacy in your marriage, beware pointing that "accusing finger" at each other.

I'm not saying you need to stuff your feelings. She doesn't have to like his dropping dirty clothes anywhere; he doesn't have to like her thoughtless spending. But neither do you have to eat from the Tree of the Knowledge of Good and Evil by judging—that is, presuming to be like God and thereby, turning away from Him and fighting each other.

In fact, you don't have to hide behind the Law and its behavior standards, wielding judgment as a weapon to protect yourself. Instead, you can trust in your relationship with God and each other. That is, you can eat from the Tree of Life and respect yourself as much as your

Father does. You can express yourself freely by speaking the truth with grace—like this:

> "Honey, if you could put your dirty clothes in the basket, I'd really appreciate it."

Or,

> "Sweetie, I worry when our credit card isn't paid up. I'd appreciate it if you could be a little more careful with the spending."

Father God's relationship with His people is not primarily about judgment, but rather, about extravagant, undeserved love—even for the most hated and outcast of this world, much less for your beloved spouse. "Long before he laid down earth's foundations," in fact, "he had us in mind, had settled on us as the focus of his love, to be made whole and holy by his love…. He wanted us to enter into the celebration of his lavish gift-giving by the hand of his beloved Son" (Ephes. 1:4-6TMB).

And so, "Anyone who believes in him will never be put to shame" (Rom.10:11).

We don't have to do it right in order to earn God's love; in fact, He loved and died for us "while we were yet sinners" (Rom. 5:8). His unbounded blessing in the full face of our sin-nature is the hallmark of the Father's heart. In fact, *His love empowers you to do it right*—even as it empowered Jesus' ministry thousands of years ago.

That's grace.

Husbands and wives, please: try to make such grace the hallmark of your heart for each other. If only because His sacrifice was so costly, God hopes that we'll honor His example by in turn giving grace to each other.

TO SHARE HIS GRACE

It's not that we first have to perform and only then receive His grace, but rather that we're so grateful for His undeserved kindness that we *want to share* His grace with others—even, especially, with your beloved!

Not judging each other gives Holy Spirit free rein to bless a couple. So we have to ask: Why do we husbands and wives do it?

According to the dictionary, *to judge* means "to act as a judge, to pass judgment, to decide upon critically." So here's the key: *Judging someone does not reflect high standards for yourself, but low respect for the other.* As such, it can come from "looser" as well as "tighter" standards—as, for example, "You're so rigid and compulsive about organizing everything!"

In fact, you can even judge someone for judging! How's this for the ultimate: "You're so judgmental about everything and everybody!" —?

It doesn't have to be that way. How's this: "Honey, when you label me like that, it makes me feel judged and boxed in. It's hard for me to listen to you when I just want to protect myself" —?

We may judge others for not sharing your politics, your morality, or your work habits, but we can also judge others for not having your taste in music, food, or reading. Or we can focus on another person's looks, clothes, and car. The word *prejudice* literally means to *pre-judge*, that is, to label someone negatively before knowing them—as in racism, sexism, and ageism.

It doesn't really matter what the issue is or which side you're on; it's easy to become judgmental toward anyone who's different from you. And let's face it: men and women are different.

A woman, for example, often must learn to multi-task as a mother, wife, and career woman; a man is usually more singularly focused, as on his job or sports game. Women can talk and feel at the same time;

a man often retreats into his "cave" to think about a situation before talking.

So when differences come up between you, I say to the woman: give your husband a little time by himself to think things over before pressing for a "conclusion." To the man, I say: sit down and listen to your wife tell you her feelings and perceptions without interrupting or leaving.

In his book *Respectable Sins: Confronting the Sins We Tolerate*, Jerry Bridges lists "judgmentalism" as one of fifteen sins that we too often tolerate in ourselves. "The sin of judgmentalism is one of the subtlest of our 'respectable' sins," he declares, "because it is often practiced under the guise of being zealous for what is right."[10]

So what's wrong with being right? The same thing that's wrong with telling the truth without grace. "God gave the Law through Moses, but grace *and* truth came through Jesus Christ," as John puts it (Jn 1:17, italics mine).

TRUTH + GRACE

The truth can stir shame and pain. If you want your spouse to listen to your truth, offer it humbly, with grace. Confessing your own related shortcoming is a good way to start: "Honey, I know I'm not always good at doing this myself, but I'd appreciate it if you could (do such and such)."

Maybe your spouse parks in the garage so it's hard for you to get your car out. You don't have to say, "You always park your car in my way!" and imply judgment that he/she is a bad driver. You can say, "I know that garage can seem pretty tight sometimes and I may not always give you much room. Could we both work at leaving a little more room for each other when we pull in?"

Judgment always comes as a "speaking down" to the other person; grace comes with humbly "speaking up" together. "There is no difference at all," as Paul declared:

> *Everyone has sinned* and is far away from God's saving presence. But by the free gift of God's grace *all are put right* with him through Christ Jesus, who sets them free. (Rom. 3:22-24, italics mine)

If you need any more motivation to speak with grace, note that the New Testament warns twenty-two times not to judge. "Do not judge others," as Jesus declared, "and you will not be judged. For you will be treated as you treat others. The standard you use in judging is the standard by which you will be judged" (Matthew 7:1-2 NLT).

Let's face it: living with a judge is no fun; you're always on trial, threatened with consequences: "If you don't (do it how I want it done), I'm going to (make you pay)." No one wants to be on trial. The court focuses on accusing and building your case against the other; *marriage focuses on encouraging each other and building a case for the two of you together.*

Upholding the Law is about truth and punishment; upholding your marriage is about the grace and blessing which build relationship. Often, in fact, the judged person will simply judge back in defense. "That critical spirit has a way of boomeranging," as Paul warned (Rom. 7:1 TMB):

"So you think I'm a slob? Well, you're nothing but a wasteful spendthrift!"

And down the hole they go. It's the devil's poker game: "I'll see your judgment and raise you mine."

At the same time, grace without truth—as in always overlooking without ever acknowledging the other's sin—can seem cheap, as it often comes from a fear of being punished for speaking your mind.

Such enforced "niceness" leads to suppressed anger that's looking for a chance to explode.

Yes, love and wisdom may at times require taking your anger to Jesus only and leaving it with Him, praying for your spouse and sometimes never speaking about it at all. But if not speaking up becomes your default—as a "policy" *based on fearful distrust of the other rather than a timely grace based on hopeful trust in God*— sooner or later an enemy spirit of anger will come knocking.

In that case, being judged can make you passive-aggressive. That is, you may pretend to agree and yet lash back secretly to irritate your partner without fear of retaliation.

It can get nasty. For example, one wife told me she threw away one of each pair of her husband's socks to "drive him crazy." A husband said he left a photo of a female bikini model open on his computer screen where his wife would see it.

In order to escape judgment, we flee intimacy.

I know it can seem hard to talk about what's bothering you. But experience will teach you that it's a lot easier than pulling apart and nursing your anger.

Nothing kills love in a marriage like the fear that comes with being judged. "There is no fear in love," as John counters. "Well-formed love banishes fear. Since fear is crippling, a fearful life—fear of death, *fear of judgment*—is one not yet fully formed in love" (1 Jn. 4:18 TMB italics mine).

UNCONDITIONAL LOVE

The judgments of our human sin-nature undermine the unconditional love in your altar vows, "for better or worse." Like Adam and Eve, we believe the Snake's original lie not only that God is holding out on you, but so is your spouse. "If you really loved me," we imagine, "you would do it my way"—and then judge your partner for withholding and not doing it your way.

In fact, no husband and wife meet each other's expectations completely. Even what was once endearing in the early stages of a relationship can later become annoying or frustrating, which may lead to judgmental thoughts and comparisons. You may have loved the way the other was so spontaneous in the beginning, but later you become frustrated that he/she is "irresponsible" and can't book that vacation trip in advance.

Such disillusionment is a common stage of marriage, which can arise out of silly little things such as the other's personality quirks or annoying habits. It says: "I love you—but only when you do what I want or expect."

Judging your partner like that stirs shame, which disconnects you and makes you withhold love.

OK, so how can you stop this destructive pattern?

It's helpful to remember that your judgments often are based not on facts, but on your own preferences, assumptions, or even shortsightedness, rather than any inherent "good" or "bad" quality of what you're judging. In order to curb your judgments, therefore, try to separate the facts of a situation—the who, what, when, where and how—from your evaluation of it as being good, bad, stupid, rude, boring, crazy, etc.

Without that rational perspective, it's easier for your emotions to get hooked and you judge the other person, either to protect yourself from disappointment or punish him/her for it.

For example, a woman whose father was absent in her girlhood may be overly sensitive to feeling abandoned by her husband, as, "You're so selfish, you just do whatever you want and never tell me." A man whose mother was possessive or "clingy" may be overly sensitive to feeling controlled by his wife, as, "You're so demanding and never give me room to do what I want."

Remember: you're not in a relationship with yourself. Your spouse is not a miniature or mirrored version of you, so he/she isn't going to think, feel, act, or believe just like you. Insofar as you can accept the other person as different from you, you can embrace those differences and accept the other person as he/she is. It's a basic part of love.

In the above examples, the husband can be more deliberate about sharing his plans and being sure to make time for his wife as well; the wife can tell her husband what she would like him to do and why she would appreciate it, then trust him to do it.

GUT REACTIONS

As you begin to check your gut-level reactions, you can begin to reframe the situation and give your beloved the benefit of a doubt. Think: "You're not trying to sabotage or undermine me. You're not purposely trying to upset me. You're a different human being doing it the way that seems best to you."

The enemy tells us to use judgment as a weapon against your partner, so he/she will back off and you won't be so stressed. But you soon find out that judgment only ups the ante, causes your partner to run away or lash back, and increases your stress.

I'm not saying you need to tolerate words that hurt and actions that harm. Each of you may need to call Time Out once in awhile. You can set boundaries, however, without judging the person. It's one thing to say, "You're a cruel and abusive person!," another to say, "I'm feeling threatened right now, and need to pull away to protect myself."

When you can set aside your judgments, life situations become less stressful for you—not just with your spouse, but with your children, and even waiting in the checkout line at the store or dealing with rush-hour traffic.

As you learn to be more accepting, you'll experience how marriage reflects the radical acceptance God has for us all. In fact, God loved us "while we were yet sinners" and sent His Son to win us back to Himself and to His plans for us (Rom. 5:8). The Father sees our wrongdoings, but doesn't record them; He wants you to love your imperfect spouse even as He loves imperfect you.

"The Lord is merciful and loving," as the Psalmist says,

> slow to become angry and full of constant
> love. He does not keep on rebuking; he is not
> angry forever. He does not punish us as we
> deserve or repay us according to our sins and
> wrongs.... As far as the east is from the west,
> so far does he remove our sins from us. As a
> father is kind to his children, so the Lord is
> kind to those who honor him. He knows what
> we are made of; he remembers that we are dust.
> (Ps. 103:8-14)

Similarly, the Father's love "endures forever"; His "steadfast love never ceases, His mercies never come to an end; they are new every morning" (Ps. 118:1-4; Lam. 3:22,23RSV). God never gives up on us. So instead of judging, He wants you to love your partner with that same faithfulness.

"Love is patient and kind," as Paul reminded the Corinthian church:

> It is not jealous or conceited or proud;
> love is not ill-mannered or selfish or irritable;
> *love does not keep a record of wrongs*; .... Love
> never gives up; and its faith, hope, and patience
> never fail. (I Corinth. 13:-7 italics mine)

The Old Covenant in Moses is about obedience to the Law and maintained by the threat of punishment and promise of reward. The New Covenant in Jesus is about trusting relationship with Him and maintained by the Father's undeserved favor—which makes you *want* to do what He has said is best for you and for your marriage.

When times get tough as a couple, surrendering to the Father and trusting His grace allows Him to transform your heart (see Rom. 12:1). That's how His "listen to her" word to Gordon changed everything in our fight (Chapter 3).

Without God's grace, we're lost; with it, all things are possible: "Let us then approach God's throne of grace with confidence, so that we may receive mercy and find grace to help us in our time of need" (Hebrews 4:16 NIV).

BITTER ROOT JUDGMENTS

It's hard, because the wounds are often deep. Most of us learn to judge at an early age. You may have heard "bad girl!" or "bad boy!" when your parents didn't like your behavior. Often, however, you weren't trying to do something evil, but just exploring and learning about your world and relationships as normal part of growing up.

Eventually, you went to schools that graded your conduct and performance based on preset group/class expectations rather than on your own particular learning style and creative gifts. Judgment, whether spoken by a teacher or implied by test results, often goes with education—even as later, with jobs, playing sports, and other performance-based activities.

As an adult, therefore, it's easy to judge your husband/wife—and also your children.

Again, it all began with Adam and Eve. It's part of life since we ate from the Tree of Knowledge; none of us escapes either judging or being judged, both of which hinder your ability to receive and to give love.

So go easy on yourselves. For most of us, learning not to judge takes time and effort.

Remember: you're most likely to judge someone else and demand payback when you feel hurt or wounded. That's precisely the time when you need most to surrender your feelings and circumstances to Jesus. "We need love most when we deserve it least," as the saying goes.

For example, my mother was very critical of me as a child, and I resented it. I also judged her for the way that she criticized my father. I made an inner vow that I would not be like my mother. Yet, I often found myself becoming critical of my family in the same way.

In order to stop repeating this generational pattern, I needed to forgive my mother. I did that in prayer, starting by telling Jesus how much her judgments hurt me. Before long, I was crying as the pain poured out of me.

Eventually, when those tears had softened my heart, He showed me that she, too, was judged by her mother (my grandmother). When I saw my mother with Jesus' eyes of compassion, I cried for her own wounds and forgave her—even prayed for her to be healed. At last, Jesus showed me a "critical" spirit in my female bloodline; I cast it out of me, and asked for His spirit of mercy, which enables me now to bless my family and others.

Jesus warned that you'll be judged by how you judge others. Thus, if you judge your spouse, that opens the door for him/her to judge you similarly—as in the above examples of dropping dirty clothes and overspending. It goes both ways; if you want mercy when you hurt others, don't judge them when they hurt you.

To head off this vicious cycle, ask the Father to search your heart and show you each judgment that you've made against your spouse. Ask God to forgive you so it doesn't fester in your heart. While you're at it, live boldly: ask your spouse to forgive you, too!

CURSE IS BROKEN

You can do that because on the cross, Jesus bore, and thereby canceled the punishment we deserved for judging others. When you realize that Jesus has saved you from the Law's death sentence, what can you do but worship Him? In that humility, you can ask for the blood of Jesus to cleanse your spouse from all effects of your judgment, and dedicate your heart to bless him/her instead.

As Paul declared, "The Spirit of life in Christ, like a strong wind, has magnificently cleared the air, freeing you from a fated lifetime of brutal tyranny at the hands of sin and death" (Romans 8:2TMB).

Since Jesus' sacrifice, that is, we no longer have to live under the curse of judgment from the Tree of Knowledge. Instead, we can live freely under the blessing in Jesus, the Tree of Life.[11] That means a couple can experience together the fruit of God's Spirit: "love, joy, peace, patience, kindness, goodness, faithfulness, humility, and self-control" (Galat. 5:22).

When you're surrendered to Jesus, you don't care about being right; you just want to be real, because you know, as Gordon says, that if *you're real before Jesus, God will make you right.*

As you cry out to Jesus and let Holy Spirit do this renewing work in you, a new freedom opens up. What used to upset you doesn't any more. The spouse whom you just fought tooth and nail against can once again become your best friend. Like any other miracle, I don't understand it, but I can testify that it happens.

When you're no longer trapped in right-or-wrong thinking, you can let go of judgments. You can turn your major focus from what's wrong with each other to what's good. You can love and connect together with compassion and understanding.

Best of all, you can remember what first turned you on to each other in the first place.

As Paul urged,

> I'd say you'll do best by filling your minds...on things that are true, noble, reputable, authentic, compelling, gracious— the best, not the worst; the beautify, not the ugly; *things to praise, not things to curse....* Then the God of peace, who makes *everything work together*, will work you into his most excellent *harmonies.* (Philippians 4:8,9NLT/ TMB *italics mine*).

Give the Father your desire for control. Determine to seek in your spouse "things to praise, not things to (judge)." Surrender your disagreement to God, ask for His wisdom how to deal with it, and trust Him for "his most excellent harmonies" in His time and way. Accept your spouse as he/she is *right now in this moment* without trying to change, manipulate, or coerce. Trust that your partner is doing the best that he/she can and trust God to lead you into the best He has for you both.

Such trust helps you avoid being personally offended and labeling or judging the other's behavior as bad. It also frees you to pray for him/her sincerely and powerfully.

FIGHTING ON THE SAME SIDE

Seeing your spouse non-judgmentally, you can discuss your issue and even offer constructive advice without getting hooked by your own past wounds and feeling offended.

"It's okay—we're fighting on the same side" as Gordon often reminds me.

Take time to remember why you fell in love with your partner. Look for and focus on things you like about him, her positive qualities and loving ways. Remember when you first met, look at your history together in photographs, read a past romantic card or love letter. Listen to your favorite "love song."

Here's the bottom line: When a human being gets married, he or she is still human and therefore, imperfect—not in just one but in many ways. Once you accept this reality that we're all imperfect, the Accuser/Evil One loses its punch. Judgments simply become unnecessary, and it's more important to work for that "excellent harmony" which the Father of you both has not only designed for you, but whose Spirit empowers in you.

"Summing it all up," I'm often reminded that out of all the men in the world, my husband picked ME out of all the women in the world to marry—and with whom to spend the rest of his life. In that realization, I'm grateful for how the Father has brought us "into his excellent harmonies."

We've made it hard for God at times and it hasn't always been easy.

But for me, the old Mick Jagger song "Loving Cup" says it simply:

> Yes, I'm fumbling and I know my car
> don't start… (but)…

> I'm the man that brings you roses when
> you ain't got none.

My husband and I both have to work on overcoming our self-centered human nature. But he goes out of his way for me and brings me flowers just because I like them.

I leave you with this assignment: What can each of you do to go out of your way and bless the other?

Just one place with no competing,
Just two lovers' hearts are beating.
No comparing other lovers,
Fear of failing under covers now.
That's what rings and promises can give:
Shelter from the storm where we can live,
together.
Where we're taken in just as we are,
loved with every blemish, every scar.

"Rings and Promises," song by Jim Manley

Sexual desire is a spiritual phenomenon. Sexual problems in a marriage are therefore often rooted in spiritual/emotional issues.

5

When You're Hot, You're Hot; When You're Not...

It's Time to Talk about Sex

It's good for a man to have a wife, and for a woman to have a husband. Sexual drives are strong, but marriage is strong enough to contain them and provide for a balanced and fulfilling sexual life in a world of sexual disorder. The marriage bed must be a place of mutuality—the husband seeking to satisfy his wife, the wife seeking to satisfy her husband. Marriage is not a place to "stand up for your rights." Marriage is a decision to serve the other, whether in bed or not. I Corinth. 7:2-4TMB

"BUT WHAT ABOUT MY sexual needs?"

Often when I speak at conferences about marriage, this question arises during the Q & A session afterward, not without frustration.

It's an excellent question, which we'll deal with here straightaway:

There's no such thing as a sexual need.

Nor, as Paul declared above to the church at Corinth, does a Christian marriage allow sexual "rights."

In our sex-obsessed, media-driven culture, those statements can draw a gasp of offense for challenging our have-it-your-way expectations.

"Give me an example of something you need," I explain, "—something you must have in order to live."

"Air…food…water…protection," come the shout-outs.

"Right. Those are needs," I note matter of factly, "—but nobody's ever died from lack of sex."

If I'm feeling particularly compassionate, I add, "I know it feels like that sometimes. But trust me. You'll survive."

Indeed, what a sad self-indictment for a husband or wife to assert a "right" to sex, as if you weren't good enough to win the other's affection! That's not making love, it's legalistic arm-twisting. Imagine a Valentine's card from your beloved with red letters: "I demand my right to sex from you!"

Not a turn-on.

In fact, the only sexual need is for both husband and wife to be surrendered to Father God and thereby, to feel safe together under His covering and free to enjoy His blessing.

We have neither sexual needs nor rights, but rather, sexual *desires*. Once we release desire from such rigid definitions, we're free to experience it more genuinely and freely (see "Naked but not Ashamed: Learning to Trust" in *Pure Sex*).

Still, it can seem unfair. God has given men and women a desire for each other. Why then shouldn't a husband or wife be free to fulfill it?

For openers, when we're talking about desire which requires another human being to fulfill, the other person's desire—or lack of it—weighs in with at least half the authority, and the plot thickens considerably.

Married Christians, in any case, should certainly be more able to fulfill sexual desire than those who don't know the One who created it. Indeed, how can you fulfill something if you don't know what it was designed to accomplish?

SEXUALITY AND GOD'S IMAGE

Knowing its Creator means knowing that sexual desire was designed to reflect His image in man and woman united physically and spiritually. That's good news, because it means the Father therefore blesses sexual union between a Christian couple, who have dedicated their lives apart from the world to Him.

Yet the Father knows how hard such intimacy can be for us in this broken world, because He knows that its brokenness lives within us all. That's why He sent Jesus: to release His Spirit in and among us—so He can overcome our self-centered nature, heal us emotionally from past wounds, "deliver us from evil," and enable us to love each other freely and fully.

In the world, that is, sexual freedom is about expressing desire however, whenever, and with whomever you want. In the Kingdom of God, *it's not about the absence of restrictions, but the presence of the Father, who enables its created purpose.*

The biblical definition of faith is "hope in things unseen" (Heb. 11:1). Fulfilling sexual desire requires such faith, because it's so often unpredictable, waxing and waning on neither partner's plan. Some want more sex, some want less—even at different times.

It's not like scheduling a business appointment.

I learned this years ago, when I worked one college summer vacation as a chauffeur for a company executive. Soon after I began, he told me I would be driving him home an hour early every Friday, leaving the office at 4 pm, because "my wife will only do it once a week, on Fridays at five." Needless to say, I quickly became skilled at navigating late Friday afternoon traffic!

Then one Thursday afternoon, my boss came to the car at 4 pm. To my surprise, he jumped in and exclaimed, "Let's go!" with his usual Friday enthusiasm.

Uncertain, nevertheless as a dutiful employee I drove off toward his home. After a few minutes, I noted delicately, "You know that today is…Thursday…right?"

In the rear-view mirror, I saw his jaw drop in dismay. With a curse, he shook his head and muttered, "I guess I got ahead of myself this week"—then told me to drive around town for another hour before taking him home.

This "disparity of desire" can cause conflict between husbands and wives, especially when we don't respect God's intention for it in the first place. Without His perspective, in fact, the world's view can easily become extreme if not ridiculous.

Thus, a *Dear Abby* column some years ago offered a tongue-in-cheek solution to the problem. "From the letters I get," she basically noted, "there's a lot of disagreement between husbands and wives on how much sex they want. Not many are happy with the status quo. About half the men and half the women who write me say they want more sex than they're getting; the other half want less.

"The disagreements, hurt feelings, and frustration are everywhere. But there's an easy way to settle this: just pair up the men who want more with the women who want more, and those who want less with the others who want less."

Husbands and wives might chuckle—or cringe—at this "solution," because we know it's not that simple. In fact, it's easy to imagine that once the "mores" all get teamed up, half of them will eventually decide they want less and half the "lesses" will want more!

IT'S DICEY

Let's face it: sex is dicey. Some times and occasions work for him, some work only for her. Even those times and occasions can change.

Sure, my boss' wife agreed to schedule their time once a week. At the risk of judging, however, it's hard not to believe she was acting more out of duty than desire. Even as I write that, nevertheless in my boss' behalf I'm moved to cite the old Willie Nelson verses, "One night of love don't make up for six nights alone/But I'd rather have one than none/'cause I'm flesh and bone."[12]

In any case, there's no on-off sexual desire switch or scheduling app which guarantees fulfillment (see "From Love Bug to Faith: Sexuality and Spirituality" in *Healing the Masculine Soul*). Emotional stress, lack of exercise, monthly biology, kids (not to mention babies), hormones, poor diet, illness, and a frustrating variety of other distractions can throw water on the fire quicker than you can say "not tonight, honey."

Beyond the physical and emotional factors which make sex dicey, however, here's the most significant factor that's rarely acknowledged: *sexual desire is a spiritual phenomenon.*

Touching a keyboard to type these words, for example, is a physical act. But a man and woman can see each other across a room without ever touching each other, and their eyes and bodies can stir— with no wire or microchip connecting them.

"There's more to sex than mere skin on skin," Paul declared. "Sex is as much spiritual mystery as physical fact" (1 Corinth. 6:16,17TMB; see "Embracing the Mystery" in *Pure Sex*).

"When you're hot, you're hot!" as the old song proclaims, then adds wistfully, "When you're not, you're not." Honest couples know how true—and often frustrating—that can be.

Sure, it's easy to wish both of you were always hot—or at least, always in sync. When you're engaged by spiritual power, however, you're simply not in control.

"The wind blows wherever it wishes," as Jesus reminded Nicodemus, the Pharisee leader trying to grasp His teaching; "you hear the sound it makes, but you do not know where it comes from or where it is going. It is like that with everyone who is born of the Spirit" (John 3:8).

It can also be like that with sex. When the wind blows in your direction, your sails are full and you're cruising. But at other times, doldrums steal the wind. Worse, it can blow fiercely back in your face.

That is, you know the feeling which desire stirs in your body, but you can't pinpoint where it comes from. By Holy Spirit's power you can exercise the self-control to focus it faithfully, but you can't always make attraction happen—or not happen—on cue (see Gal. 5:23).

SPIRITUALITY AND ATTRACTION

Respecting this spiritual nature of sexual attraction humbles you to where you can recognize and surrender to the God who controls it. "You gave us this desire, Father," you can pray together, "and we're grateful for it. But we give it up to you and ask you to focus and fulfill it in us."

"Therefore," as Paul declared, "I urge you, brothers, in view of God's mercy, to offer your bodies as living sacrifices, holy and pleasing to God—which is your spiritual worship" (Rom. 12:1NIV).

Entrusting your desire to Him allows you to respect your partner's desire as well as your own.

Our Western, rational/scientific culture, however, does not respect spirituality, because *its often overwhelming power reminds us that we're not in control.* That reality stirs the shame and fear which fuels our sex-addicted culture. Amid the urgency of desire—not to mention the emotional stakes if you're excited and your spouse isn't—we try to co-opt God's Spirit and trade our insecurity for manufactured certainty (see "Controlling Uncontrollable Desire" in *Pure Sex*).

For example, I once saw a gift catalog item called "Do You Wanna?"—a simple wooden tray with two walnut-sized chrome spheres for the couple's bedroom. If you want to make love, you simply put your sphere in a groove marked YES. Presumably, when both husband and wife spheres are in the groove, *Voila!* All doubt and insecurity is erased, and the love flows freely.

Maybe.

At least, hopefully.

Seasoned husbands and wives, however, know it just doesn't always go according to our most careful plans, even when both of you "wanna." Sometimes the unplanned happens—or the planned just doesn't. Without *trusting the Father for His larger plan,* too often the world and the enemy rush into the vacuum, stirring fear, shame, and hurt feelings, topped off with a fight for good measure.

When you don't feel aroused, that is, it's easy to feel ashamed for not being able to perform. Because sexual bonding is fundamentally a mutual experience, however, when it "doesn't happen," often each partner has a share in the problem—and the solution.

So don't beat yourselves up; instead, give yourselves up to Jesus. Pray about it together. Surrender it all out loud to the Father.

SHAME AND DISTRACTIONS

Otherwise, if you don't surrender to the Father for His perspective, it's too easy simply to withdraw from each other and cover your shame with distractions like the classic, "I have a headache." When all else fails, you can establish distance and save face by starting a fight as a diversion.

Or you can grasp after "alternatives." I once counseled a Christian couple, for example, who said they could only get excited by watching porn movies together. Others have said they fantasize some other, presumably more arousing scene than where they are.

Disengaging from reality and from each other, however, is the problem, not the solution. The joy of sex flows, rather, as you connect more fully to the Father in a spirit of thanksgiving and surrender. His love and protection defines ultimate reality, affords ultimate security, and leads to ultimate intimacy. That's what enables you to connect *more fully and freely to each other in the moment.*

Thus, in "Porn and the Threat to Virility," a startling *Time* magazine article reports a growing disorder among young males called PIED, or "Pornography Induced Erectile Dysfunction."[13] Rather than increase desire and performance, researchers discovered that fantasy sex often snuffs out male sexual response with a real woman.

One 18-year-old young man actively engaged in porn found that when he wanted to have sex with his girlfriend, "There was a disconnect between what I wanted in my mind and how my body reacted." In poignant irony, fantasy had co-opted reality; his "body only responded to the sight of porn."

PIED is graphic evidence that ultimately, *when sexuality disengages from its created purpose, it can no longer fulfill it.* This reality raises the question, profoundly unsettling to our often lust-driven culture: What if orgasm is not the goal of sex, but rather, the byproduct of its divine purpose—namely, uniting a husband and wife both emotionally and spiritually in the Father's image, even in His joy and blessing?

AUTHENTIC FULFILLMENT

Yes, human beings can experience orgasm with someone you don't know at all, like a prostitute, or even with no one else, as in masturbation. But what if sex apart from covenanted relationship with your partner and the Creator distracts from its divine purpose—and thereby, from its authentic fulfillment? It's like skipping from the first to the last chapter of a mystery book right away, never knowing the characters and missing the adventure—not to mention its full pleasure—via the complete story.

Even as Pharaoh's magicians could make snakes out of sticks just like Moses, the enemy of God can stir sexual desire (Exod. 7:8-11). In that unholy irony, the more desperately you focus on the apparent "fulfillment" of sex in orgasm, the more likely you disengage from your partner, and thereby short-circuit genuine fulfillment in your marriage.

Thus, PIED.

I've counseled both husbands and wives separately who have effectively said, "I'm tired of fighting and waiting for us to feel close. It's easier just to do it myself." When the time comes to make love again together, however, you may be distracted by fantasies. As often in life, quick fixes can preclude more lasting solutions.

Again, disengaging is a detour from genuine intimacy. Pornography and masturbation invite enemy spirits of alienation and isolation; you'll need to renounce and cast those out before you can respond freely together.

Most often, each partner approaches making love with the unspoken goal of being satisfied. In a perfect world, that fifty-fifty avenue of self-satisfaction sounds great. Between two different and imperfect people, however, it eventually just doesn't work.

That's when the "desire Garmin" in your heart eventually needs to "recalculate."

"The marriage bed must be a place of mutuality," as Paul declares in the opening chapter scripture, "the husband seeking to satisfy his wife, the wife seeking to satisfy her husband" (1Cor. 7:3).

It's simple: If indeed, each partner wants/expects to be satisfied, instead of focusing on yourself, focus on satisfying the other.

Done. You're both satisfied.

It's not just courtesy. It's love.

Our self-centered nature, however, can sabotage this "balance" and make you think the other is not focusing on you as much as you're focusing on him/her. So you turn away, pout, and withdraw. But such self-centeredness only diminishes love, and thereby, desire.

In any case, if your sexual relationship has gone south–or is heading in that direction–here's a suggestion to help you re-focus on each other, deepen your love, and rekindle the flame:

Take turns to focus entirely on pleasing just one of you. The simple concession to "ladies first" is appropriate here to manly initiative.This time, it's all about her. The husband surrenders for a later occasion all claims on getting what he wants, and instead, wants only to satisfy her. A foot rub is often good for starters. If you're not sure, try something and see how it goes; if it doesn't work, try something else.

Take plenty of time; no rush, just gentle and easy. We're not focusing on a grand finale here, but on re-building the foundation of love by caring for the other person.

Let the man learn to find pleasure in giving pleasure to her. Let the woman learn to rest in receiving from him.

When she's pleased, the woman does not now work to satisfy him, but simply rests in her satisfaction—as does he. A loving good-night kiss, and you both sleep well.

Next time, let it all be about him similarly.

After that, focus on each other and go for it together.

PERFORMANCE ANXIETY

Sure, self-focused, goal-oriented sex together can be great when you're both chafing. As a default expectation, however, it can distract you from your spouse and create a "performance anxiety" which shuts him/her down.

One Christian man, for example, told me that his fears of not responding led him to try the sex-stimulating drug Viagra.

"It sure worked," he declared, shaking his head in amazement. "I have to confess it was nice not to have to worry about all those doubts and fears."

Then pausing, he knit his brow. "But eventually, I could see how I was getting dependent on the drug and losing sight of my wife. It was starting to be all about performance and less about each other.

"And then one day I was praying and the Father said, 'Let go of the Viagra'. When something in me balked, I knew I was getting hooked on the drug and it was definitely time to stop using it.

"Still, letting go of Viagra wasn't a snap. I was scared at first because I didn't want to face whatever was driving my lack of desire. I got prayer at my men's group and saw a Christian counselor, which brought up some significant wounds from my past and some enemy spirits along with that.

"Eventually, after getting that healing and deliverance, I decided not to let shame run the show. I started talking to my wife about it and praying together. The more we did that, the more we began to understand and trust each other.

"It turned out she had some insecurities, too, and we worked on that. Before long, the desire came back as strong as ever."

Pausing in reflection, he added, "What I first thought would bring us closer—just having more sex—was actually pulling us apart *the more we tried to make it happen instead of just letting it flow.* Sure, like most couples, once in awhile it doesn't work even now like we want. But I feel a lot more connected to her, even to myself.

"We learned that sex is better when it's *something we do together, not separately in the same bed.*

"I don't judge guys who use Viagra," he said finally. "But for me, God used it as a warning of sorts, which I decided to listen to. I can only say, I'm glad I did."

It's important to note here that the dynamic this man described is not to be assumed for women. God works in our physical bodies and not just in our spirits; female hormonal functions are more complex and therefore, may require different attention.

Like a man, a woman's sexual response can often be affected by emotional and spiritual issues. Her physiology, however, adds a unique factor, not only regarding monthly periods but also as she ages and hormonal changes can become significant. A medical endocrinologist and a Spirit-filled Christian counselor and can help her navigate that process.

Meanwhile, any honest man or woman knows that self-doubts, fears, and shame can often attend desire. It makes you wonder: could such challenges be the Creator's call to welcome Him into this most sensitive aspect your life together—even to experience His grace and freedom?

When all else fails, get real with God. "Father, we want the desire you have for us," you can pray, "but all our trying so hard to make it happen is only making us feel more ashamed that it's not happening, and driving us apart.

"We give our frustration and fear to you. Please come and show us what you're doing here and how we can cooperate with you."

HOLY SENSIBILITIES

What if the Father wants most to teach you and your spouse an intimacy together beyond that of any other relationship on earth? What if He can use even your sexual fears and misunderstandings to draw you to Himself, as in the above prayer, and thereby overcome the shame which draws you apart?

After all, we're talking delicate, even holy sensibilities here as two sinners-by-nature open their bodies and hearts to each other. It's the most fundamentally mutual experience on earth, which therefore requires commensurate respect for your partner, as well as for yourself.

Amid such great expectations, great shame and fear lurk. That's why Father God wants to be welcomed into sexual desire—and must surely grieve as Christians hardly ever talk about it in church (see "Foreword" in *Pure Sex*).

When "differences of desire" arise, therefore, you don't have to pull away from each other and hide or sulk. Together, you can surrender your egos and expectations to the Father. You can let the uncertainty and even disappointments draw the two of you into deeper communication, understanding, and freedom together.

Any couple who have done this will tell you it's not always easy. Shame is a powerful emotion, which the enemy often uses to drives couples apart. But those who persevere in faith will tell you that Father God's grace is more powerful. "We surrender our sexual desire to you, Father," is a simple but foundational couples' prayer which opens the door for divine covering—and blessing.

Certainly, in this broken world, a deep and chronic inability to respond sexually may occur. While physical issues can contribute, often past emotional trauma must be addressed for healing, via counseling and prayer.

It's been estimated, for example, that one in five American women was sexually abused as a child, and one in twenty boys.[14] This wound cuts deeply into a child's heart. Later as an adult, it distorts and inhibits sexual desire. You want to bond sexually with your spouse, but your wound makes you associate sexuality with pain and fear. So in your marriage you swing back and forth from attraction to rejection—an exhausting push-pull dynamic which only causes distrust and further wounding. Again, a Spirit-filled Christian counselor can lead you into God's healing for this.

Here's the bottom line: *The more a husband and wife feel emotionally safe with each other, the less sexual performance is an issue.*

That security, however, is often determined by their childhood family experiences.

If as a girl the wife felt safe with her father and affirmed in her femininity by her mother, if as a boy the husband felt safe with his mother and affirmed in his masculinity by his father, the couple's desire for each other in marriage will more often flow naturally. If their parents were distant, rejecting, or otherwise abusive, the pain and fear from that childhood experience will afflict their desire for each other as adults.

Through Jesus, God's Holy Spirit lives among and within us to heal those childhood wounds and allow a husband and wife to enjoy each other freely (see "Healing Emotional Wounds: Seeing the Past as Jesus Sees It" in *Broken by Religion, Healed by God*).

The overriding goal for a husband and wife, therefore, is to feel safe together, so your marriage can become a *sanctu*ary. In a bird sanctuary, that is, you can't shoot at the birds. The Latin root word *sanctus* means not just "holy," but set apart, that is, a place different from the world, a zone of trust, where the world's self-centered expectations, performance, and judgments are pre-empted by the Father's love (see Lev. 20:26).

So if the spark's not there, go easy on yourselves. "Doesn't look like it's going to happen tonight," one of you can say. "That's disappointing—I wonder what's going on?" Let the other also respond, and suggest "maybe there's something we need to talk about?"

On the other hand, maybe there's nothing to talk about; it's just not happening. Leave it at that with a loving hug and simply hold each other for awhile, without judgment or analysis.

Sometimes, both of you were not really wanting to make love, but were just going along to accommodate the other. When you're struggling to make something happen together and it's not working, finding out that you both aren't really into it can be an occasion to laugh together at your fears.

At other times, one or both of you can be iffy. In those "maybe" moments, don't be afraid to give it a try. "Well, let's just hold each other and see how it goes," one of you can say.

Surprises are always at hand when you turn control over to God; sometimes the best adventures can begin with you both feeling iffy. Sure, it's risky—but what adventure isn't?

In any case, if it goes, that's great; if it doesn't go, that's great too—you enjoyed holding each other.

If you go for it and it starts good but then fades, give yourselves credit for boldly stepping out together. Give each other a hug and trust for next time. Athletes don't score every time they get a chance. But even when they don't, they stay in the game. Again, while you don't want to get too cerebral about it, talking about sex together can diffuse fears and overcome shame.

EMOTIONAL WOUNDS

Physically fit and happily married to his wife Gina, George (not his real name) came to me frustrated. "Sometimes it just flows great, and other times not much happens at all," he sighed, confused.

As we prayed over several weeks, the Father surfaced and healed many boyhood wounds from his mother and past romantic relationships that were coloring his feelings for Gina, plus wounds from his father that were affecting his masculine confidence. George learned in that process to surrender his sexual desire to Father God, release to Him any control of his responses, and walk in grace by telling the Father what he wanted but not worrying about the outcome.

"I want it to happen, Father," he prayed, "and I thank you for all the great times Gina and I have had together. But I can't make it happen. I give up—not to whatever's shutting me down, but to you, Father!"

"Don't worry about anything," as Paul encouraged the church at Philippi, "but in all your prayers ask God for what you need, always asking him with a thankful heart. And God's peace, which is far beyond human understanding, will keep your hearts and minds safe in union with Christ Jesus" (Phil. 4:6,7).

The next week, George came to our appointment with a strange mixture of joy and bewilderment. "Last night Gina and I both knew it was time," he declared, "and I was really ready.

"But all of a sudden, without any warning and when I least wanted it to happen, everything died in me. I mean, it was gone. It was frustrating alright, but I was able to stay centered and pray under my breath. 'OK, Father—I don't have a clue why this is happening, but I give it all up to you. If I can't enjoy this, help me to make it enjoyable for Gina'."

George threw up his hands and shrugged his shoulders in wonder. "I can't explain it, but a minute or two later the lights went on for me again and it was great!"

As we praised God, the Bible story of Abraham's call to sacrifice his son Isaac came to mind. I suggested to George that, as with Abraham, surrendering to the Father what he valued most and trusting Him for the outcome turned things around. If so, it was a graphic lesson in how completely sexual fulfillment is in the Father's hands.

Still, it's a mystery. This story is not about a formula for holy Viagra, but rather, a relationship between a Father and His son. Over the years, George and Gina had prayed and worked hard on their healing, both individually and together, in order to trust each other and the Father in their marriage; I believe He honored them for that.

Here's the bottom line: The emotional and spiritual roots of sexual desire mean that *sexual problems are often rooted in emotional and spiritual issues.* The emotional issues most often arise from past wounds; the spiritual issues, from being disconnected from God and influenced by ungodly spirits.

The key is to stay real and open together. Deal with any lurking shame or anger so it doesn't co-opt your desire. Sometimes, just removing the pressure to perform can free you to flow together. Remember: *Sexual intimacy is not about how hard you try, but about how sincerely you surrender to God and to each other.*

Sure, it's great when you're both excited and ready. Often, however, it can flow better if you don't rush it. Take time to know and enjoy each other. "I Want a Man Who's Got a Slow Hand," as the old Vonda Shepard song puts it; "I want a lover with an easy touch."

GIVE UP—TO GOD

A simple prayer here can be helpful: "Thank you, Father, for giving us a desire for each other. We can't just make that happen;

you're the one in control, not us. So we give up—not to our fears, but to you. This is uncomfortable territory where shame has ruled us too long, but we're trusting your grace. If there's something you want to teach us, please do; we're open.

"In any case, help us to enjoy this wonderful gift of desire that you've given us."

Meanwhile, amid the shame and fears in our sex-saturated culture, we can forget what really spurs desire for the other, namely, love. Sometimes it's helpful just to tell what you like about each other. Take time to be specific and genuine.

As most couples know, feelings can easily be hurt in this tender arena of sexual expression. That's why desire flows most freely within mutual trust. *When a man and woman feel safe together,* pulling away or shutting down is far less likely to happen. That's one reason God created and shepherds marriages: because only within the security of His covenant can partners experience the depth of trust and thereby, safety and freedom which His covering provides (see "Sexual Bonding and a Woman's Heart" by Mary Dalbey, in *Pure Sex*).

As a *sanct*uary, the *sanct*-ified covenant of marriage is designed to provide a place apart from the world, where Father God has supreme authority. Under His Kingdom rule, you can be real together and not judged or shamed. Surrendered to God, you can be loved and accepted "just as you are" with no "fear of failing under covers"—as the song lyrics "Rings and Promises" before this chapter.

The more open you are together, the more important emotional safety becomes. And let's face it: no other human experience makes us more vulnerable to one another than making love. When a man and woman open their bodies to each other, their hearts open as well. "Words of love" and other blessings register deeply; slights or criticism which in any other context might be overlooked become sirens which short-circuit intimacy.

That's why when conflict rises up between you, desire flees. Sadly, many couples hide their wounds and never seek healing; they just shut down, and eventually can't remember when they last made love.

Remember: both husband and wife bring their sin-nature into the marriage. Sooner or later, you're likely to disappoint and hurt each other in your sexual expectations. That's why the Father sent Jesus: to offer His mercy in *an ability to forgive*, and His grace in an ability to bless each other even after such wounding.

If you think that sounds unreasonable or even impossible, I say from my natural human view, you're absolutely right. But Jesus says this: "With human beings, this is impossible, but with God all things are possible" (Matt. 19:26NIV).

And so I urge husbands and wives: fall on your knees together before your Father, confess how you've hurt each other and ask forgiveness from Father God and each other.

Have you judged or criticized your partner's "excess" or lack of sexual desire? Have you allowed your differences and disagreements to harbor anger or resentment? Are the two of you willing to pray together, talk openly, and if necessary get help from a Christian counselor in order to heal your wounds and resolve your issues?

MARRIAGE AS SANCTUARY

Ever since Eden, our human fear of not measuring up to the Father's call becomes entirely justified; in fact, in our own willpower we can't even trust Him to empower us. The shame of that inadequacy infects our sexuality—and can rise up when a husband and wife want to become more open and intimate together.

That's why the Father has designed the marriage sanctuary. In Jesus, He has overcome that shame and opened the door to His heart. A Christian couple, that is, can go to the Father and give Him their fears of inadequacy and worries of not performing.

That means you can sit down together, hold hands and agree, "Let's get this awful shame off our backs from the get-go. At different times, each of us will fall short of the other's expectations. Both of us won't always be 100% ready and willing."

Confess that, accept that, and agree to love each other no matter what. On the count of Three, say together, "I'm scared I won't perform." Then hold each other and say, "That's OK. So am I. But I love you."

Then get on with the adventure.

A final note: Traditionally, as with the former boss I chauffered, it's been assumed that the man is frustrated and wants more. More recently, however, the ideal of "sexual equality" has revealed its downside in that often women are now just as likely to be left wanting.

"It's flat-out unfair," as one husband declared to me in a couples' ministry session. "A woman can have sex whether she's into it or not. But a man has to get aroused or nothing happens. The whole burden is on him to perform."

"You just don't get it," his wife cut in. "I have to feel close to you to be aroused and enjoy it—or I don't want it at all!"

"You always say you want to get closer," the man shot back. "Well, I feel closer to you when we have sex!"

This couple love to fight. If instead, they would fight to love, they would know the power Father God gives them to win together.

So we interrupt this argument for a commercial from the Creator.

No, not by might, nor even power,
But by your Spirit, O Lord—
Healer of hearts, binder of wounds,
Lives that are lost restored;
Flow through this land,
til woman and man
Sing praise to your Name once more.

"Not by Might," (adapted) song by Robin Mark[15]

> **Rational insights are helpful to reveal the roots of your anger, but only Holy Spirit can uproot it—and heal its damage.**

6

Hurt People Hurt People

But Holy Spirit Heals

*He heals the broken hearted and binds up
their wounds.* Ps.147:3

SOME YEARS AGO, a couple came to me for help—call them Sam
and Sally. The tension was heavy as they sat down, so I cut to the
chase.

"What seems to be the problem?" I asked.

As both sat tight-lipped, I waited.

"She's always angry at me for something!" Sam burst out finally.

"I am not!" Sally shot back, teeth grinding. "You just…you just
frustrate me so much!"

Without going into details, I'll just say the conversation went
downhill fast from there. I tried my best. I gave each of them three
minutes to sound off without the other firing back in return. But the
battle just heated up.

Very soon, I realized that I had no idea how to stop the fighting between them. Eventually, in frustration myself, I shrugged uneasily.

"Listen," I offered, "you're both really angry at each other, but if we're going to get to the bottom of this, I suggest for now that you take a break from the fighting. How about the two of you go to Disneyland this weekend together? Get away from the home scene awhile, then come back next week and we'll see if we can start off better."

Certainly, that "therapy" wouldn't have earned any points from my pastoral counseling professor in seminary. But it was all I could come up with at the time.

The next week, the approaching appointment with Sam and Sally began to stir uneasiness in me—which was confirmed when they came into my office and both fell silent but fuming onto the couch.

Clearly, Mickey Mouse had not done the job, not even at the Happiest Place on Earth.

"OK…," I began hesitantly. "How…did it go at Disneyland?"

"It was awful," Sam leapt in. "She started yelling at me even before I got out of the driveway. 'Don't turn here! Watch out for that car! You're going too fast!' She never let up once."

Sally sat listening intently, eyes narrowed and brow furrowed.

"So what did you do when Sally was saying that to you?" I asked.

Sam paused. "Well, …I guess I just shut up. I mean, I was afraid anything I said would make things worse. I just didn't know how to stop her."

I turned to Sally. Strangely, at Sam's statement, her expression had given way to an empty sadness. Rolling her eyes, she shook her head slowly from side to side.

"OK, Sally," I offered fairly. "Now it's your turn to express yourself to Sam."

Dropping her head, she sighed deeply. "It's true," she said finally, "I was awful."

Startled, Sam and I both sat up and stared at each other in confusion. I was OK with letting husband and wife take turns venting their anger against the other, but clearly we were about to leave the Pastoral Counseling class far behind.

"Well...," I began, stumbling ahead. "Sally, could you maybe just...tell us what you mean?"

OUT OF CONTROL

Sally sighed again, then looked up at Sam. "Honey," she managed, "I was...I was out of control. I needed you to help me get back in control again. But you just shut down and ran away from me. You abandoned me when I needed you to be strong and stand with me.

"When you pulled away, it made me even more mad at you until I just...just couldn't stop myself."

Jaw agape, Sam stared at his wife. Leaning forward, he opened his mouth to speak.

"I know what you're going to say," Sally interrupted, "—that if you spoke up I'd just jump on you more. Maybe, I would have," she allowed thoughtfully, "—but I needed you to stay with me and not give up."

Stunned, I shook my head in silent wonder. This scenario was not in any marriage counseling textbook I'd ever read, Christian or secular. Clearly, my 50-50 vent-your-feelings technique had bottomed out. I had no idea where to go from there.

"Sally...," I offered tentatively, "I really appreciate your being so honest and open. But I need you to help us out here. What could Sam have done or said back then in the car that would've helped you 'get in control again'?"

Softer now, Sally shook her head again sadly. "I…I'm not sure," she murmured. Disarmed and humbled by the unknowing, we talked and eventually agreed on some things Sam could have said to help Sally:

"I want to listen to you, Sally, but I'm so frustrated myself now that I need some time to pull myself together. Can we call a halt just now, not talk for just a few minutes, and then try again?"

Or he might say, "I know you're really upset just now. I want to hear what you're saying, but I'm spending all my energy defending myself. Could we maybe pull over to the side of the road for a minute and I'll do my best to listen. It would help me do that if you could tone it down a bit."

I told this story at a women's conference not long afterward, and asked them for suggestions. "Sam could've just said, 'That's enough!'" one woman declared. "'Stop what you're doing and think about what you're saying!'" Many of the other women there nodded in approval.

I have no magic answer to what Sam might have said to help Sally control herself. I only know what she told him, that pulling away from her communicated neither strength nor love, but rather, abandonment.

Neither lashing back nor shutting up, that is, brought healing. Both are basic animal fight-or-flight responses, which bear no power to reconcile and transform. Clearly, a third, preeminently human response was needed to face the issue and resolve it together.

With that goal, I suggested a question for each to jump-start the process.

Sally said she needed Sam to be stronger and not weaker. "Why did you withdraw when Sally got angry," I asked him, "instead of standing and helping her face what was upsetting her?"

Sam needed Sally to become more gentle and not so critical. "Why did you get so angry at Sam when you were in the car on the way to Disneyland?" I asked her.

CHILDHOOD WOUNDS

As I suspected, the answer to both of these questions lay in their childhood families.

Predictably, Sam reported that as a boy his parents fought often and bitterly in front of him. "Usually, Mom would start yelling and cut Dad down so bad that he'd grab his hat and leave," he recalled. "Most of the time, that's the only way the fighting would stop.

"But really, when Dad left, Mom only got madder. Sometimes, she'd even turn it on me and say, 'You're just like your father!'"

Sam never saw his parents resolve conflict by talking things out directly with each other. His masculine model in Dad told him later as a man himself simply to run when the woman got angry. When confined in the car with Sally, he couldn't leave physically, so he just clammed up and turned away from her—which only made her feel abandoned, and therefore, even more angry.

Sally, in turn, grew up in a similarly frustrating environment. She watched her mother become furious at her father and cut him down with criticism, and he would shut down in silence. But she, too, saw how her mother's frustration only exploded more when he disconnected from her.

As an adult herself, her mother's model of womanhood told her to expect to be abandoned by the man in her emotions. When Sam did that by clamming up, it tapped that reservoir of pain from her girlhood, and she lashed out at him as her mother had done to her father.

These insights helped Sam and Sally understand how they were getting hooked into such anger, and allowed them each to own their part in the wounding. But the impulse to fight remained, and I was not able to lead them into a deeper freedom from it.

As their pastor, I confess that I had no idea beyond rational insights how to help Sam and Sally stop fighting. At that time, I had not met Holy Spirit and experienced the fullness of God's power. Some time later, however, when I received the baptism of Holy Spirit, I found the missing dimension of power to my ministry—and faith (see "My Battle Partner—The Paraclete" in *No Small Snakes: A Journey into Spiritual Warfare*).

After that, another couple—call them John and Jane—came to me with similar family histories, and I was able to help them work together with Jesus for deeper and more lasting healing. When they saw at last how their childhood family wounds were repeating in their own marriage, they were determined to break this destructive generational pattern.

We prayed and invited Jesus to come in the power of Holy Spirit and lead the way. Taking turns, I encouraged John first to close his eyes and ask Holy Spirit to bring to mind a particularly painful memory of his parents' fighting. After a few moments, he remembered a time at "about five or six years old" when "Mom and Dad were shouting at each other."

INVITING JESUS INTO PAIN

As his face grimaced at the pain, I asked him to invite Jesus to come and stand beside him as his parents fought. John did so, and we waited. Eventually, in his mind's eye, he saw Jesus "standing there with me."

I then told John to thank Jesus for coming when he cried out, and to tell Jesus that He was free to do or say anything He wanted. Soon, John told me he saw Jesus walk over to his parents, stand between him and them, and raise His hand for them to stop.

When the parents fell quiet, Jesus explained to them how their thoughtless fighting was scaring little John and He wanted them to stop. After listening to Jesus, they bent down, picked him up, and hugged him. "I'm so sorry we hurt you like that," they said. Soon John was crying, sobbing tears from boyhood pain pent up for decades.

When he stopped, I instructed John to ask Jesus, "Show me my mother and father as you see them." After a moment, he realized they had both seen their own parents (John's grandparents) fight similarly, that they were just doing themselves what they had each been taught by example—and re-creating their own childhood wounds in him.

This truth set John free.

"I forgive you, Dad and Mom," he said out loud, "for frightening me so bad and not caring about what you were doing to me. I realize you were just acting out of your own pain from your own parents.

"I forgive you for teaching me by example to do the same destructive thing in my own marriage. And I pray that you'll go to Jesus like I'm doing, so He can heal you from your wounds."

Finally, John realized he was not to blame for his parents' dysfunction. Sure, Jane had hurt him. But John couldn't grow beyond his lingering anger and outbursts at Jane until he faced his own boyhood wounds and asked Jesus to heal him.

After that healing, he could withhold lashing back at Jane or running away. Instead, he could express his feelings to her with less of an "angry edge," and even consider her feelings without the extra baggage of his own childhood pain and anger. That enabled him to talk openly and freely with her about their problem without accusing or shaming. "It really hurts when you do that," he was able to tell Jane. "How can we work together to change this pattern?"

When I prayed for Jane, she also called out for Jesus in a painful memory of her own parents' fighting. "I don't see Jesus like John did," she said, "but I can feel He's here." I reassured her that when you call on Jesus, He comes whether you see Him or not (see Matt. 18:20). I then encouraged her to step out in faith, thank Jesus for being with her, and then in His presence proceed herself to speak up to her quarreling parents.

"Thank you for being with me, Jesus," she said. Then, after a moment, she stepped ahead in faith.

"Mom and Dad, stop fighting so much!" she burst out. "You scare me when you do that and don't even care about what that does to me! You make me feel worthless, like my feelings don't mean anything to you."

Soon, Jane began to cry, and after a moment, I encouraged her to call out for Jesus again. She did so, and reported that she felt His arms holding her.

I encouraged her to ask Jesus, "Show me my parents the way you see them"; like John, she saw both her mother's and father's similar childhood pain and wept for them. She could then forgive them in the presence of Jesus, naming specifically the behaviors which had wounded her so deeply. That allowed her to release herself from the grip of anger and bitterness that colored her view of John.

ENEMY HOOKS

But we were not finished. The fact that John and Jane were so easily hooked into anger toward each other suggested that the enemy had leveraged their wounds. When Jesus had healed their emotional wounds, no hooks remained for the enemy to manipulate the two of them into wounding each other like their parents. The final task was now to identify the enemy spirits fueling their fights and cast them out.

I then led them in a prayer calling for Jesus to come and oversee this deliverance (see *A Couples' Guide to Spiritual Warfare*). Their previous prayers for healing wounds were at times angry, but focused appropriately and humble. Now, facing combat with the enemy, we needed to shift gears and pray boldly and decisively.

First, we asked Holy Spirit to come and reveal the names of spirits which had capitalized on their wounds. Eventually, as they recalled their parents' fighting, the names *anger*, *revenge*, and *bitterness* came to mind.

Next, I invited them to pray something like this:

"Thank you, Jesus, that you died on the cross so we could receive the power of your Spirit today, thousands of years later, and walk in your victory. Thank you that you came 'to destroy the works of the devil', that you who are in us are greater than he who is in the world, that by the power of your Spirit we don't have to keep wounding each other as the generations before us (1 Jn 4:4).

"In the name of Jesus, we declare to you anger, revenge, and bitterness that you are trespassers in our lives, in our marriage, and in our family. We renounce your presence and influence in us. We are son and daughter of the living God revealed in Jesus, to whom you're nothing but a 'footstool' (Ps. 110:1).

"Forgive us, Father, for allowing this evil in our lives and even cooperating with its destruction.

"In the name of Jesus, we set the cross between ourselves and our parents, between them and their parents, and on back through our bloodlines. And we speak to you now in Jesus' name and command you anger, revenge, and bitterness to get out of us now and go directly into the hands of Jesus!"

We waited a moment to sense this had been accomplished. At one point, an extra "holy shove" seemed necessary, and I encouraged them to pray simply, "Jesus, remove these spirits from us." At that, both John and Jane felt a distinct "sense of release."

Having evicted the evil spirits, we now needed to re-occupy their hearts with works of Holy Spirit. "What would you want in your lives and marriage instead of anger, revenge, and bitterness?" I asked John and Jane.

We came up with several answers: mercy, grace, love, compassion—which the two then asked for from the Father. With that,

I prayed a blessing to seal this work of God's Spirit in their hearts and marriage, and sent them on their way relieved and smiling.

More work was needed to heal other wounds between them. But this upending, saving encounter with Jesus demonstrated that the power was at hand to do it.

We're ready now to look more deeply at how we project your childhood bonding to Dad and Mom—or lack of it—onto your marriage. We'll see how Father God's Commandment to "honor your father and mother" frees you from past wounds to focus on "the land you are about to occupy"—that is, the unique marriage He's designed for you both (Exod. 20:12).

'Cause I am your lady,

and you are my man;

Whenever you reach for me,

I'll do all that I can....

We're heading for something,

somewhere I've never been.

Sometimes I am frightened,

but I'm ready to learn

The power of love.

"The Power of Love," song by Celine Dion 1986

> The childhood fantasy that your parents were perfect is idolatry. When you grow up, it keeps you from honoring them genuinely and from growing in God's purposes for your marriage.

7

Leaving Father and Mother

The Trailhead to Marriage

For this reason a man will leave his father and mother and be united to his wife, and they will become one flesh. Genesis 2:24

Respect your father and mother, so that you may live a long time in the land that I am giving you. Exod. 20:12

THE PREVIOUS STORIES SHOW how your parents' relationship imprints on your heart and shapes your expectations of marriage—for better or worse. That reality is clearly grounded in the Bible, as above, literally from the beginning of time.

At first glance, each of these two scriptures seems clear on its own, yet contradictory together: How can you leave your father and mother and also respect them?

Only by God's leading.

In order to join with the woman according to God's will and reflect thereby the image of God, the man must "leave father and mother." Since this injunction focuses on bonding sexually as "one flesh," clearly the woman shares in it—and to that extent, must leave her own father and mother as well.

This simple fact of life is not a call to disrespect your parents—which would break the Commandment to respect them—but rather, to grant primary loyalty and faithfulness to God. It's not about rebellion, but idolatry; that is, worshipping or attributing identity and saving power to your parents instead of to God.

To understand this, imagine if I could have talked with you when you were in your mother's womb:

ME: You're about to enter this world as a child, so I want you to know God.

YOU (in the womb): What do you mean by "God"?

M: God is the One from whom you come. God loves you, surrounds and protects you, feeds you, talks to you, listens to you, and provides for your needs. God is with you more closely than anyone in the world.

YOU: Oh, I understand now. God is this woman who carries me, in whom I live and move and have my being.

This life-defining impact of the mother-bond can hardly be overestimated. Whether you acknowledge it or not, it's organically "known" to your body and spirit. When you were in her womb, whatever your mother ate, you ate. What she felt, you felt. When she was anxious, her body chemistry and nervous system communicated that anxiety to you. You were not *apart from* her; you were literally *a part of* her.

The natural, primal state of human life is to be one with the mother—and ultimately, to confuse her thereby with God. That's why so many pagan spiritual practices include goddess worship.

This reality is so common, even universal, that it's subconscious. At the very genesis of creation, therefore, God warns clearly that it must be acknowledged—that the couple must "leave father and mother," *lest subconscious childhood loyalties pre-empt His plans for the two of you.*

But the confusion doesn't stop with Mom's womb. Outside and beyond her, another compelling voice, often deeper and stronger, beckons. Lacking the graphic physical connection as with your mother, your father's voice and presence nevertheless stirs with a *spiritual* recognition or connection. (see "Foreword" to *Do Pirates Wear Pajamas? and Other Mysteries in the Adventure of Fathering*).

Thus, the father re-defines you as not just part of your mother, but in fact, *apart from her and thereby, a part of* the larger world. Even as the mother bond typically draws you into the security of relationship, the father bond draws you outward into purpose and destiny.

Certainly, most of us can point to positive characteristics of your parents that you want to carry with you throughout your life. Nevertheless, in order to fulfill God's calling on your marriage, the natural bond to both mother and father must yield to the *super*natural bond with Father God.

Mom and Dad, that is, might be compared to a booster rocket which propels you out of their world/power sphere and into your own life orbit. The booster rocket then drops off, leaving the space module to navigate by itself via the larger powers of energy from the sun and gravity from the earth. Similarly, leaving your Mom and Dad means navigating your life now via the security that God provides, the purpose for which He created you, and His power to walk it out.

MATURE DEPENDENCY

That mature dependency upon God enables Him to create your own, unique family as an adult with children, via bonding as "one flesh"—and allows you to discern His created purpose for you and your spouse, distinct from your parents.

It's basic to life on this planet, even archetypal—like the old frontier wagon train. That pioneer journey begins with a bugle call to destination and sets out accordingly in a straight line—a masculine image. For protection, as at night or when under attack, the wagon train draws into a circle—a more feminine image. Within that secure place, the pioneers draw strength in relationships. Together, they share meals and stories, heal the day's wounds, fix the wagons, play harmonicas and sing songs, shoe the horses, and are restored for the journey ahead.

In the morning, the cycle repeats as a man sounds the bugle and the circle of wagons breaks out once again from a circle into a straight line toward its destination.

Thus, the basic model of femininity focuses on security, and of masculinity on destiny. Clearly, both are necessary to the journey—and thereby reflect the complete image of God when bonded. Without security and relationship, the pioneers lack protection and reason to live, and die; without a purpose or destiny, the journey lacks focus and doesn't accomplish anything.

Certainly, a mother can sense and pursue a vision for herself and her family, and a father can desire to protect his family and build relationships together. But this gender model in the wagon-train can be helpful when differences arise between a husband and wife.

A healthy marriage, that is, *enjoys both security and a sense of purpose for the partners*. At the very creation of man and woman, therefore, God declares, "It is not good for the man *to live alone*"—thus, to provide security in relationship—and concludes, "I will make a suitable companion *to help him*"—thus, to invoke destiny via pooling their energies after a common purpose (Gen. 2:18, italics mine).

This classic difference sparked conflict between Rick and Rita, a couple in their late 30's with three children, who came to me frustrated with each other. They had been living in a smaller house for some time, which left Rita exasperated at "having everything packed in with no room to turn around." A possible new job had come up for Rick that would make a larger home possible, but he was worried it would be "too humdrum" with "not much chance for trying new things."

With a thin smile, I shrugged and shook my head in surrender. "Welcome to man and woman together," I sighed with a smile. "Rick wants adventure and Rita wants security. That's how life is for a man and a woman. This is where you learn to honor each other for the sake of the wagon train/family and negotiate your needs so you fulfill God's destination/purpose."

From that larger view, I asked the couple, "What if God established your marriage so Rick could learn to appreciate the security in a home together, and Rita could learn to value the adventure of trusting God more deeply and taking risks?"

Often, in fact, *what attracts you most to your spouse is the very thing that frightens you most about him/her.*

"I really do like the focus of being in our home with the family," Rick eventually confessed. "I guess I'm afraid if I give in to Rita on that, I'll lose my excitement and passion for new adventures."

"It's true," Rita chimed in with a wry grin. "I can get pretty ingrown sometimes and afraid of trying new things. I do like the excitement when Rick gets me out of the house to take walks and do things I wouldn't do myself. But sometimes I'm afraid he'll take us all off to some Neverland where anything at all could happen."

BALANCING PERSONALITIES

When we prayed about it, each thanked God for the "scary" but helpful trait in the other, then asked God for wisdom how to balance their personalities and desires for the larger good of the family. Both Rick and Rita needed to leave their natural comfort zones—not only for mutual respect, but in order to accomplish God's greater purposes in their marriage.

Significantly, the Genesis exhortation that a couple must leave the natural security of their childhood came before The Fall. Afterward, once humanity became infected with a self-centered sin-nature, that ingrown impulse to stay with Dad and Mom—whether physically or emotionally—has passed down to us all.

Unto today, it can keep husbands and wives from growing up together.

Meanwhile, because of our inborn impulse to worship our parents, seeing them as imperfect can stir shame in a child. What's more, that natural parental bond is enforced by a fear that, "If Daddy and Mommy are not all-powerful, they can't protect and provide for me."

In any case, to a child it seems both more loyal and safer to deny your parents' weakness and whitewash their shortcomings. That's addictive denial, motivated not by respect but rather, by shame and fear.

To whatever extent that this childish view remains unchallenged— that is, insofar as the man and woman do *not* leave father and mother— their marriage will be contained and restricted by their childhood experience. In fact, each of you may remain a child by recreating your parents' marriage—even in its painful and destructive aspects.

A boy and girl do not a husband and wife make. Marrying and starting a family, however, impels you subconsciously to migrate back to "family" as Mom and Dad defined it. The word "*family*," in fact, shares the same root word as "*famil*iar"; what felt familiar and at home for you as a child beckons you later when via marriage you start your own home/family.

If Mom and Dad argued often, for example, conflict feels "at home" for you as a child. Later, as an adult, you'll expect and may even start fights in your own marriage to re-create subconsciously that *famil*iar experience, and its false comfort. Similarly, for example, if your opposite gender parent died, left the family, or was emotionally unavailable, you'll be naturally drawn to a partner who is either emotionally distant or even physically absent.

Yes, Jesus blessed child-like humility as the gateway to the Kingdom of God (see Matt. 18:1-5). But anyone who can remember third-grade recess knows that kids are not always so innocent, and in fact, can be decidedly unkind to one another.

Child-like is about humility and trust, which foster relationship; child-ish is about self-centeredness, which destroys relationship. Any honest husband or wife knows how child-ish-ness can create conflict in a marriage.

In fact, the more child-like you are before God, the less child-ish you are with your spouse. That's why from our very Genesis as a species, God wants us to know Him as our Father—*which requires leaving your parents.*

In fact, faithfully "leaving father and mother" enables you to incorporate the good which Mom and Dad gave you, and to outgrow the rest.

BLACKMAILED WITH SHAME

Because your childhood experience defines family for you, however, it can feel shameful to see anything wrong with it. It's tempting tell yourself instead that your parents were basically OK, if not perfect.

That way, you can avoid facing their humanly negative qualities—even as those qualities wounded you as a child and manifest painfully as an adult in your own marriage. Within that lie, the father of Lies binds you to childhood—and thereby blackmails you with shame for "saying bad things about your parents."

God's goal, however, is not to curse or scorn your parents—as my "hippie generation" did in the 1960's—but rather, to "respect" them, as the Commandment. Thereby, God promises that you will enjoy a "long" life—that is, free of anger or bitterness toward your folks and able thereby to see your own husband/wife more clearly (Exod. 20:15).

The childish fantasy that your parents were perfect is idolatry. It hides you from the often uncomfortable truth that would set you free as a mature adult to love your spouse. Facing your parents' shortcomings with grace for their circumstances allows you similarly to face gracefully your spouse's shortcomings—and your own.

It thereby frees a couple to face their need for Father God.

Acknowledging that your parents were/are entirely human and therefore, card-carrying sinners, requires facing that you and your spouse are also. That confession opens the door to compassion and mercy in your heart not just for your parents, but also for yourself—even, indeed, for your spouse.

From that "place of grace," at last each of you can forgive your mother and father for their faults and appropriate their finest qualities as your blessed inheritance. In fact, you can genuinely respect them—*not because they were perfect, but because they did the best they could amid their circumstances and sin-nature*, even as you struggle to do so amid your own.

That humble respect engenders God's promise of a long and blessed life.

In fact, it's how you grow beyond a natural child of the flesh into a child of God. "For through the living and eternal word of God, you have been born again as the children of a parent who is immortal, not mortal," as Peter declared (1 Pet. 1:23).

What's even better, facing and taking your childhood family wounds to Jesus can teach you the major lesson of fighting in the Spirit: that power is at hand to forgive and be forgiven.

"There is no difference at all," as Paul declared, "everyone has sinned and is far away from God's saving presence. But by the free gift of God's grace all are put right with Him through Christ Jesus, who sets them free" (Rom. 3:24).

"Everyone" includes Mom and Dad, even as you and your spouse.

Your parents, that is, were not gods, but sinners just like you and everyone else in this fallen world. If you doubt that, wait until you become a parent yourself and examine honestly your own actions toward your children. As a human parent, you're bound to hurt your child in some way.

So why not be bold in the Spirit? Ask the Father how you've hurt your child. If in doubt, when they're old enough to respond, ask your children themselves to tell you how you hurt them. Don't defend yourself; respect their feelings and just listen. When the Father and/or your child has spoken, demonstrate that you heard what was said by naming the offense and humbly asking his/her forgiveness—like the previous examples of reconciliation between husband and wife.

Such honesty takes courage—the kind that frees a family from anger at each other to focus instead on what God's doing in their lives..

HONORING YOUR PARENTS

For an adult, honoring your parents requires compassion. It's about appreciating the reality of their struggles and respecting them for doing the best they could with what they had. Such grace motivates you in turn to do the best with what you have.

What's more, you can forgive Mom and Dad, release them to God, and bless them. You can then let Jesus heal your childhood wounds, face your own family/marriage struggles, and welcome Him into your own circumstances.

Respect for your mom and dad—as for any other human being—begins with simply accepting them for who they are, for better or worse. It means not trying to force them into your image of what you wanted or even needed them to be, nor waiting for them to change.

That's the difference between idolizing your parents as a child and respecting them as God intends. It allows you responsibly both to honor them and to pursue your own destiny together with your spouse and Jesus.

It's called growing up.

As a "hippie rebel," I wasted years of my young adulthood struggling to change my parents instead of begging God to change me and see them with His eyes. My disrespect and ultimately fruitless efforts blinded me to the dysfunction in my own adult relationships. In fact, it delayed my "entering the land" God had prepared for me to occupy with Mary as my "suitable companion" (see "Hippies, Fathers, and Forgiveness" in *Sons of the Father*).

Struggling to change your parents not only breaks the Commandment to honor them; it doesn't work, because it's most often fueled by anger and the grandiosity of hiding your own shortcomings. As Mary warns in her chapter about judgment, that's a bad precedent for when you marry.

Worse—and this clearly betrays the enemy's fingerprints— focusing on "how Mom and Dad did or didn't do it" in the past distracts you from how Father God wants to do it now. Ultimately, it keeps you from recognizing and working together to fulfill His call on your life.

The more you "leave father and mother" by seeing them not as a child, but with Jesus' eyes, you can see and know your spouse uncolored by childhood expectations. That means the more genuinely you can love your partner as he/she really is, and the more securely you can join forces in fulfilling your destiny together.

Thus, in the previous chapter, John and Jane found healing and purpose together only after facing squarely the wounds their parents had inflicted. In that process, they saw at last how their parents were themselves wounded as children.

That vision stirred the compassion in John and Jane necessary to forgive and respect not only their parents, but each other as well. Rather than divide their families, facing their childhood wounds opened a new level of respect for their parents and intimacy with each other.

It's called grace. It doesn't happen without Jesus, simply because our human sin-nature doesn't allow it.

We like convict and restrict; Jesus likes confess and bless.

Here's the takeaway: If you haven't faced how your parents wounded you and forgiven them sincerely in the name of Jesus, it can be hard for you to deal mercifully with others when they wound you—especially your spouse. Eyes clouded by leftover judgment and pain from childhood will distort how you see your spouse.

Years ago, a man in his 80's stood before one of my men's conference gatherings and warned us, "Whatever you don't forgive your father for, you'll do to your son." The room fell hushed as the profound impact of that statement sunk in.

PRICE OF UNFORGIVENESS

Similarly, I would offer this warning to couples: Whatever you don't forgive your opposite-gender parent for, you'll likely hold against your spouse.

For example, if a man judges his mother as controlling, he needs to believe that his wife is controlling in order to feel "at home" with her and perpetuate his struggle against his mother. When he asks Jesus to heal the wound that caused him to judge his mother, he can forgive her—and thereby, free himself to see his wife as she really is, "for better or worse." That mercy toward his mother frees a man to get on with his adult life as a husband, even to pray for his wife's shortcomings and to enjoy her attributes.

Similarly, if a woman judges her father as distant and abandoning, she needs to believe that about her husband in order to feel "at home" with him and remain emotionally bonded to her father. When she asks Jesus to heal the wound that caused her to judge her father so, she can forgive him—and thereby, free herself to see her husband more clearly, "for better or worse." That mercy toward her father frees a woman to honor her father, get on with her adult life as a wife, even to pray for her husband's shortcomings and enjoy his attributes.

We also tend to treat your spouse according to your same-gender parent's model. If a girl's mother was critical toward her dad, as a wife later the girl may be drawn to belittle her husband similarly. If a boy's dad was disengaged from his mother, as a husband later he may isolate from his wife.

Certainly, your parents each had good qualities, and you want to receive that blessing as part of your heritage and exercise those qualities in your own marriage. The goal is to affirm, retain, and enjoy your parents' positive qualities and seek healing for the negative ones—like John and Jane.

When ministering to a man about marriage problems, therefore, I can usually get his attention by saying, "I know the name of the first woman you ever loved." Often this draws a puzzled look in response, as if to a supernatural revelation.

"Let me put it another way," I offer. "If I were to ask you as a little boy, 'What's it like to love a woman?', with what woman would you get your experience to answer that question?"

A thin smile tells me we're tracking. "I guess that would be Mom."

It's similar when I minister to a woman: "I know the name of the first man you ever loved"—and then, "If I were to ask you as a little girl, 'What's it like to love a man?', with what man would you get your experience to answer that?"

"With Dad, I suppose," comes the eventual response.

It's true. In fact, a man's experience with his mother shapes his expectations of what it's like to open his heart to a woman and love her; a woman's experience with her father shapes her expectations of what it's like to open her heart to a man and love him.

If Mom were reasonably accepting, affectionate, encouraging, and respectful toward her son, a sense of being significant and loved by her becomes fixed in his emotional hard drive. He thereby grows up expecting and indeed, seeking a woman who makes him feel that way. He won't feel at home with a woman who's critical and/or distant.

Similarly, if Dad makes his daughter feel significant and loved, she grows up expecting, and therefore seeking a man who does that. When some guy approaches her who's belittling and/or distant, she won't feel at home with him. She'll simply turn away and seek a man who makes her feel like Dad did.

While the opposite-gender parent shapes expectations with the opposite sex, the same-gender parent often shapes your own sense of gender identity. A boy in secure relationship with his father grows up secure in his manhood. He enjoys being a man and feels confident in a woman's presence. Likewise, a girl in secure relationship with her mother grows up secure in her femininity. She enjoys being a woman and feels confident in a man's presence.

FAMILY AND FAMILY-AR

That security, joy, and confidence contributes significantly to a healthy marriage later. When it's lacking and you don't take these deep wounds to Jesus for healing, the marriage suffers. You view your spouse and marriage through the pain-and-disappointment lens of your childhood glasses and often project onto your spouse the same negative expectations as with your opposite gender parent. It feels family-ar, and in that sense, like home.

"Why does she think I'm trying to dominate her so often?" a husband may ask. Often, it's because his wife's father dominated her as a girl.

"Why does he accuse me so often of being critical of him?" A wife may ask. Often, it's because her husband's mother criticized him as a boy.

"But what I'm saying about my spouse is true!" you may protest. Sure, most of us, for example, can be domineering or critical at times. In some measure, that's part of human nature. But if you experienced this as a child from your parent, any discussion or confrontation with your spouse over that issue is colored by childhood expectations. That means *it's likely to spark anger far out of proportion to the incident at hand.*

Here's the bottom line: for a child, relationship with the opposite gender parent is so deeply rooted that the parent defines love—for better or worse. As you begin looking for a marriage partner, that means you seek, often unconsciously, to recreate with your spouse how you felt with your opposite gender parent. It's just natural to do so.

The world knows this. The old barbershop quartet song "I Want a Girl Just like the Girl That Married Dear Old Dad," and the 1950's Peggy Lee hit, "My Heart Belongs to Daddy" make the point.

The bond with your opposite gender parent is your default. It's not simply heartfelt; it's organic.

Fully half a man's genetic structure comes from his mother. It's not that he's *like* her; but that to that extent he *is* her. That inward, organic identity bears an emotional imperative to bond outwardly in marriage with this "other half" of himself, as we often call the wife.

Hence, a man must face and resolve any negative feelings toward his mother so he doesn't project those feelings onto his wife.

Similarly, half a woman's genetic structure comes from her father. It's not that she's *like* her father, but to that extent she *is* him. That shared organic identity bears an emotional imperative to bond successfully with this "other half" of herself. A woman must face and resolve any negative feelings toward her father so she doesn't project those feelings onto her husband.

A cardinal rule of marriage is simply this: Wives: your husband is not your father; husbands: your wife is not your mother.

HEALING CHILDHOOD WOUNDS

This misconception fuels many a fight, simply because it's all too natural to make your spouse pay for how your opposite-gender parent wounded you—or criticize your spouse for not giving you what that parent gave you. *Once you go to Jesus to heal this childhood wound, however, you don't need to act it out any more in your marriage.*

Because the parents' relationship defines family for their children, this definition imprints on a son's and daughter's heart. That's why, for example, a girl who was abandoned or abused by her father is drawn to a man she sees as emotionally distant or abusive; a man who felt controlled by his mother is drawn to a woman he sees as clingy or demanding.

Too often, however, simply acknowledging the unhealthy "connection" to your childhood pain doesn't proceed to facing how those wounds affect you today. Indeed, a healthy marriage requires that whatever dynamics may have led to conflict between your mother and dad, even divorce, must be faced and reconciled in yourself.

A word of reassurance: This destructive dynamic doesn't mean you married the wrong person. It means you *are* the wrong person yourself—each of you—until you let Jesus heal and grow you up into the "right" or true person He made you to be, and thereby, into this marriage the Father designed for you.

Such spiritual/emotional growth between a husband and wife is an ongoing process. It starts with enjoying each other, which opens your heart, which makes you more sensitive to each other, which stirs hidden wounds of the past, which triggers conflict, which forces you into the arms of God together, which allows Him to heal you more deeply, which enables you to enjoy each other more freely.

That's often the "life cycle" of a growing marriage, grounded in a faith that Jesus is present in the power of His Spirit to grow you up together in that process.

TRUTH AS SURGERY

Like life, a healthy marriage requires facing the truth about how your childhood wounds affect your marriage. But it also requires grace, which enables you—and your spouse—to hear that truth. Without grace, love is easily eclipsed by angry accusation such as, "You're just like your mother!" or "You're just like your father!" With grace, love is enhanced by compassion, such as, "What your dad/mom did really hurt you, didn't it?"

God's Word is as true now as it was at the beginning of time. You must honor your father and mother in order to honor the part of them that is you *and be released from the wounding in their shortcomings to honor your spouse.* Furthermore, you must leave your father and mother in order to enjoy and grow in your own marriage as God intends, even to "enter the land" which God has designed for you "to occupy." Often, that entails confessing a spirit of idolatry toward your mother and father, and casting it out.

It can be hard. But I can say from blessed experience, it's worth it.

In fact, it's the pathway to new life together. Thus, we're not only born "physically of human parents," but enabled as well by the Spirit of God to be "born again" as Jesus insists, and thereby to "see the Kingdom of God" (John 3:3,6).

I want to see God's Kingdom rule in my marriage. Learning to honor my father and mother was the first step. In that grace, I could forgive them for what they didn't give me, leave them with gratitude for what they gave me, and faithfully focus my energies on my own marriage.

I'm eternally grateful that Jesus made that possible.

"Now that you've cleaned up your lives by following the truth," as Paul concludes,

> love one another as if your lives depended on it. Your new life is not like your old life. Your old birth came from mortal sperm; your new birth comes from God's living Word. 1 Peter 1:23 (TMB)

> Money exposes your values. That's why it's a
> fundamental issue of faith—and so explosive
> for couples.

8

For Richer or Poorer

Whose Money Is It?

*Remember that it is the Lord your God who
gives you the power to become rich.* Deut. 8:18
The love of money is the root of all evil.
1 Tim 6:10

FROM "10 MONEY MISTAKES that Can Ruin a Marriage" to "Top
6 Marriage-Killing Money Issues," the Google listings at "marriage
conflict finances" paint a grim picture.

"Financial issues are the primary reason for 90 percent of divorce
cases I handle," a prominent Washington, D.C., divorce attorney
declares in an article "Money and Marriage Issues: The New Rules
for Couples"[16]:

> But it isn't necessarily the amount of
> money a couple has that tends to trip them up.
> It's the differences in their spending habits and

especially their lack of communication (italics mine).

"Wife joining the workforce wants her own bank account," as a *Dear Abby* column headlined. "Until now," the husband writes, "I haven't resented her for not working because she has been caring for our children, our home, and has been a full-time student, but the thought of her wanting to keep her own money to herself is weird and hurtful to me. How can I bring this up with her without it making it seem like I think she owes me something?"

With characteristic kid gloves and a bit of humor, Abby responds, "Ask your wife why she wants to separate your finances, because marriage is supposed to be a partnership. She does 'owe you something'—an explanation."[17]

Staking out your "own money" is an issue for men, too. "My wife and I argue a lot about finances," another husband writes to a financial advice columnist in my local newspaper. "Whenever I work overtime at my job, I feel like I should be able to put my overtime pay toward my spending money. What do you think?"[18]

Whatever you think about this wife's and this husband's issues, their concern over who owns the money seems universal today. Indeed, it demonstrates how powerfully our human sin-nature can co-opt the larger picture of family needs and make communication difficult, if not risky.

"Money is a core issue for most couples," Christian financial advisor Steve Glaeser of Woodland Park, Colorado, told me. "I've worked with thousands of couples over the years, most of them Christians, and finances are the root of more divorces than any other issue."

How did money become a major cause of divorce? Why does money stir such deep, unmanageable division and even hostility? Indeed, what power does God give Christian couples to resolve those issues?

RECENT HISTORY

A partial answer to these questions may lie in recent history, where powerful social dynamics have forced finances onto the marriage table as never before in human history.

In the not too distant past—in my own parents' generation, married prior to WWII—most husbands worked at a paying job outside the home and made the money which supported the family. In return, wives were expected to stay at home, clean the house, cook, care for the children, and manage the family's social life. Not uncommonly, the man would give his paycheck to the woman and she would disburse it, presumably in the family's best interest, as for food and clothing.

Needless to say, this arrangement left plenty of loopholes for disagreement if not heated discussion. The wife depended entirely upon her husband for money, and upon his generosity for her spending. While she might prioritize her children's needs above all else, her own needs—and desires—could easily be overlooked.

Since the man made the money, that is, he naturally claimed authority over how it was spent—and feared her overspending. "With a woman, there's only two kinds of money," I once heard an older man grumble, "—hers and ours."

That earlier dispensation led men to fear that the woman might seize authority over the family finances. One older man's advice to me as a boy was blunt: "Don't let your wife get a job. If she has her own money, she'll get power over you."

Just the other day—over sixty years later—I saw a bumper sticker on a man's car to parody the one on armored bank cars: "This Vehicle Carries No Money: Driver Is Married."

"I wish I was single again," went a men's ditty I heard as a boy, "'cause when I was single, my pockets would jingle/I wish I was single again."

Growing up in the 1950's, I heard another older man say that on the dollar bill the Secretary of the Treasury seal always bore a woman's signature, because "women are better at spending money than men."

Apparently, there's some concession to this view among women. In Cathy Guisewite's *Cathy* cartoon strip, Cathy decides she needs to curb her spending and goes to a Shopaholics Anonymous meeting. As the women sit in a circle, one confesses tearfully her "uncontrollable urge" to buy new clothes.

"Does anyone have any questions?" the woman leader then asks.

"Where did you get those adorable shoes?!" Cathy blurts out.

Not to be outdone, men's overspending is acknowledged in the saying, "What separates the men from the boys is the cost of their toys."

During the Great Depression of the 1930's, for example, my grandfather was thankful to maintain his job as a steelworker; a regular workweek meant 10 hours a day, 6 days a week, with only Sunday's off. My father told me that his dad once bought a car—in those days something very few men of his social class enjoyed. It was a new, high-end model to boot, though he rarely if ever went out of town and could only drive it on Sundays. Dad said his mother criticized his father harshly for such "a waste of money" when "more important" things were needed for the family.

OVERSPENDING AND DEPRIVATION

It would seem that for both men and women, overspending reflects *an unfulfilled childhood desire to reward yourself or otherwise overcome a sense of deprivation* (see "The Commandment to Enjoy vs. the Spirit of Deprivation" in *Religion vs Reality*). In any case, money clearly stirs deep emotions—which if not faced and resolved can easily kindle a fight.

In an article "How to Stop Fighting with Your Spouse about Unnecessary Spending,"[19] the author quotes financial planner Lauren Lyons Cole, "It's a lot easier to approach this conversation if you can do it with numbers instead of emotions…. Forget emotionally loaded words like 'frivolous'."

In any case, WWII largely ended the family financial hierarchy with the man as "breadwinner." With so many men fighting overseas, women were needed in the work force at home.

Before the war, my father studied shorthand and bookkeeping for his B.S. in Accounting, and worked as an office secretary. During the war, he served as a Navy officer on an aircraft carrier, while women took over his position and others vacated by men at war. Only after WWII was "secretary" considered a woman's job.

The children of this war-shaped generation became known as Boomers. These post-WWII daughters grew up with great expectations as they entered womanhood amid the 1960's feminist movement, which upended the traditional family finance model.

Neither Mary's mother nor my own ever worked at a paying job outside the home; Mary and my two sisters have all done so matter-of-factly, even at executive-level positions.

In general, few Boomer women grew up with a mother who worked as a professional or envisioned a life of her own independent of husband and children. The culture's model of female submission and self-denial led many Boomer daughters to disrespect their mothers and even femininity as Mom defined it.

Without mothers to mentor them in the new, post-war freedoms, Boomer women sought to dissociate from Mom. This "credibility gap" between women and their mothers paralleled that between sensitized Boomer men and their more emotionally distant, soldier fathers. In a single generation, gender role models were dismantled more deliberately and on a broader scale than ever before in human history (see "She Left Me!" in *Healing the Masculine Soul*).

Family finances have also been affected by a significant increase in divorce, which often can require single women to support themselves and, as single moms, their children as well.

Certainly, a woman who has supported herself will be appropriately assertive in a marriage discussion of finances. Decisions can no longer made by male fiat, but rather, require negotiation and respect, even compromise. This cultural upheaval signals a massive shift from law to relationship—something few Boomers learned to negotiate from their more role-bound parents.

NITRO AND GLYCERIN

"Two independent professionals who marry and are used to paying their own bills, as is common today, can be like nitro and glycerin," as Glaeser declares. "Frankly, very few couples agree on finances and very often they are polar opposites in their views."

From an historical perspective, therefore, a broad range of hot-button financial issues is suddenly on the marriage table: who pays the bills, who can spend what amount without agreement from the other person, his money-her money-our money, views about debt, saving, investing, and more.

The name of the game is still "Marriage and Money," but no one knows the rules anymore.

It's a recipe for conflict.

Formulaic "solutions" in this modern dispensation can no longer be assumed. "I know this is heresy," Glaeser allows, "but my experience working with thousands of couples is that budgeting often just doesn't work. Only about three in a hundred use a budget successfully, and in every case the woman controlled the finances."

Where autonomy is an issue, he says, keeping separate checking accounts works better, recommending the couple agree on a limit amount above which "one party must get permission from the other to spend (except for agreed expenses like rent and utilities)."

To avoid conflict, he endorses author David Bach's system: "Put everything on autopilot/auto draft from your checking account: charitable giving and tithe fund, rent and utilities, insurances, debt service, saving for emergency fund, vacations, short-term goals, retirement, and such. These goals can be calculated. Spend the rest."

A variety of financial advisors today offer helpful ideas to navigate this challenging new order—or indeed, lack of it—in marriages today. What's "best," however, apparently boils down to whatever works for the two of you. It's all about your relationship now and not some traditional, pre-determined norm.

And that, of course, is why it's so hard.

So I say first to the husbands and wives of today's New Financial Dispensation: Go easy on yourselves. This is uncharted territory, filled with uncertainty and not a little fear. You're pioneers, facing an emotional frontier rarely if ever conceived of before in human civilization—one with few maps and even fewer credible explorers.

As always, for Christians the silver lining in such challenges is simply that *the less certain we become about how to do it, the more deliberately, if not desperately, we seek the God Who does it.*

So let's get the record straight here.

Many people believe that the Bible says "money is the root of all evil."

Not so. "*The love of* money is the root of all evil," Paul tells his prodigy Timothy (1 Tim. 6:10, *italics mine*).

Like most other material things, money is not evil in itself, but rather, takes value according to how you use it. For example, money can save people from poverty, hunger, and starvation, or it can fill the pockets of the rich; it can buy life-saving medicine or life-destroying street drugs.

MONEY EXPOSES VALUES

"Money exposes your values," as my friend Lutheran pastor Rev. Joe Johnson puts it succinctly. "That's why it's such a hot-button issue for couples."

One spouse may value a new carpet; the other wants a new car. For one, a large bank account means security; another isn't bothered by a small bank account if it allows for a more open-ended lifestyle.

Perhaps like no other thing we use, money often communicates power and esteem. In the world, the question "How much is he/she worth?" is answered by how much money that person has. "He's worth millions," we might say of a businessman.

In the Kingdom of God, meanwhile, the question of your worth is answered clearly by Jesus on the cross: You're a son/daughter of the King. Nothing in this world is worth more to the Creator of the Universe than you.

When Jesus was asked whether people should pay taxes to the pagan Roman government, he pointed to a coin and asked, "Whose face is on this coin?" When everyone answered, "Caesar," Jesus simply stated, "Give to Caesar what is Caesar's and to God what is God's" (Matt. 22:21).

According to Jesus, the debate over money—if not free-for-all fighting unto divorce court—is quite simply about ownership. Does that mean He sides with you when you fight for your "own money"?

Not at all. For Jesus, the battle for ownership is not between husband and wife, but rather, between the couple and God. He did not come to proclaim the kingdom of husband or the kingdom of wife, but rather, the Kingdom of God.

Where He rules, therefore, the issue of finances is not merit, but idolatry. *It's not about what you deserve, but about Whom you serve.*

The "*love* of money," that is, anchors the enemy of God within and among us. That means couples must be very prayerful and discerning about entering discussions about finances, aware that seductive powers of dominion and division lurk here.

Sure, in this physical world you need money enough to eat and pay living expenses. The border between provision and idolatry, meanwhile, lies at the juncture between two worldviews.

"I work for my money," one voice asserts, "and therefore, I have the right to spend it any way I want." Clearly, this view disregards the larger needs of the family—not to mention the larger responsibility Christians bear to support God's mission to a needy world.

"God has provided me the means to make money," the other voice confesses, "and therefore, I look to Him for how I spend it." Thus, God reminds His chosen people after rescuing them from slavery in Egypt, "Remember that it is the Lord your God who gives you the power to become rich" (Deut. 8:18).

In a marriage, the latter view requires first humility—and then honest discussion, even spiritual discernment regarding God's will for both incomes.

TIGHTWAD KILLJOY?

Often, the rub here lies in a false image of God—propagated therefore by the enemy of God—as a tightwad killjoy in the sky. "If I let God direct my finances," goes the caricature, "He'd make me give it all away and I'd live in poverty like a monk, never having any fun."

That's simply not the God of the Bible. Yes, God wants us to be generous with those in need—not out of guilt, but out of gratefulness for His generosity to us. He wants to spread the blessing and give us good things so we'll have more good things to give others.

"Command those who are rich in the things of this life not to be proud," as Paul urges his young apprentice Timothy,

> but to place their hope, not in such
> an uncertain thing as riches, but in God,

who generously gives us everything for our enjoyment. Command them to do good, to be rich in good works, to be *generous and ready to share with others.* (1 Tim. 6:17-19, italics mine)

This Father likes to bless His children with good things, even to enjoy His blessing so much that we want to share it with others. He's given us a capacity for pleasure, and the blessing to enjoy it within His boundaries. That's why biblical festivals, which commemorate His saving acts, often include rich food and even wine, as Jesus provided at the wedding in Cana (see John 2:1-12).

When God first instructed His people to tithe, He didn't mean putting check or cash in the Temple offering plate. Rather, as appropriate for a largely agrarian society, He meant giving food from your farm.

But it wasn't just the difference in currency that sets God's original view of tithing apart from our view today. Get ready to be startled as you read this:

If the place of worship is too far from your home for you to carry there *the tithe of the produce that the Lord has blessed you with,* then do this:

Sell your produce and take the money with you to the one place of worship. *Spend it on whatever you want—beef, lamb, wine, beer—and there, in the presence of the Lord your God, you and your families are to eat and enjoy yourselves…* in order that you may learn to have reverence for the Lord your God always. (Deut. 14: 24-26 italics mine)

Let's be honest: It's hard "to have reverence" for a stingy god who delights in depriving you of pleasure. Thankfully—in spite of that slanderous portrait painted by religion—that's not the God revealed in Jesus.

That means it's not the God who upholds your marriage.

"Set exciting goals together first," as Cole suggests. That is, "Inject what could be a frustrating conversation about finances with positive motivation by discussing what's in your ideal future together—fully funded college accounts? A 4-bedroom home? … That's a more effective way to talk about this than just 'cutting back,' which is just kind of sad and hard."

MONEY GOOD OR EVIL?

Money, therefore, is good when it's appreciated as the undeserved gift of God; evil insofar as it's appropriated as your own—and therefore blinds you to His generosity, even to His heart for others in need (see "Of Jogging and Cat Food" in *Broken by Religion, Healed by God*).

When I was a boy, coins were made of copper, silver, nickel, or gold. The coin's value was simply the market value of its metal content. A quarter, for example, was made of twenty-five cents worth of silver; a nickel coin was larger than a silver dime even though it was worth less.

Paper money back then was marked, "Silver Certificate" or "Gold Certificate"—which meant that for every bill printed, an amount of precious metal equal to the printed money's value was stored by the government. Today, since abandoning the "Gold Standard" in 1976, the "value" of a dollar depends entirely on the confidence which users invest in it.

Money no longer has the intrinsic value of precious metals, but rather, only the value which users attribute it. As co-users, couples therefore need to discuss, if not confess what money means to each of you: Security? Esteem?

Do you fear not having money? Why? Is it hard for you to trust God's provision?

How did your parents deal with finances together? How does that affect your spending today? As a child, did you feel deprived? Were/ are you upset that your parents didn't give you the material things you wanted? As an adult, do you feel like you deserve more than life has given you? What would it take to increase your trust of each other and consider family needs before your own?

Take time together as a couple to discuss these questions. Be sure to listen until you understand what money means to each other. Then pray together and ask God for His wisdom to guide you in your spending. Be sure as well to search your hearts for any "love of money" that would mislead you away from God's purposes.

SPIRIT OF MAMMON

In the Bible, the word "money" is often translated from the word *mammon*, which doesn't necessarily mean currency, but rather, a worship of or focus on material things as an ultimate value. As you pray together, be alert to a spirit of *mammon*, which fuels that idolatry—and yet thrives today amid our buy-it-now, consumer-focused economy.

Yes, saving money can be necessary to pay for future plans, and spending it can be a necessary investment. But beware of *mammon* if you sense any unreasonable compulsion either to hoard or to spend money—that is, if you won't buy anything for pleasure even when your budget allows it, or if you buy too much when your budget doesn't allow it.

Above all, ask God to search your hearts for a self-focused spirit of *mammon*. If convicted, ask His forgiveness for not trusting Him to provide your material needs and for not confessing that the money you have comes from Him.

Then renounce and cast *mammon* out of you in the name of Jesus. Ask the Father to replace it with His Spirit—of trust in His provision, of gratitude with what He's given you, of generosity to share it with others in need, and of wisdom to spend it according to His will.

"No one can be a slave of two masters" as Jesus declared; "he will...be loyal to one and despise the other. You cannot serve both God and money (*mammon*)." (Matt. 6:24).

With your finances, being loyal to God and to each other is all about trusting the Father to guide you as together you surrender your money and material resources to Him.

Give Him a chance.

Jesus loves children because, like Him, they restore innocence to an awfully guilty world. The question for Christian parents is simply, Will we let our kids do that for us adults?

9

Staying Focused as Parents

Whose Child Is It?

At that time, the disciples came to Jesus asking, "Who is the greatest in the kingdom of Heaven?"

So Jesus called a child, had him stand in front of them, and said, "I assure you that unless you change and become like children, you will never enter the Kingdom of heaven. The greatest in the Kingdom of heaven is the one who humbles himself and becomes like this child. And whoever welcomes in my name one such as this, welcomes me.

"If anyone should cause one of these little ones to lose his faith in me, *it would be better for that person to have a large millstone tied*

*around his neck and be drowned in the deep
sea."* Matt. 18:1-6, italics mine

I'VE SHOWN HOW marriage fights are often rooted in idolatry of
your parents. As an adult, having children yourself intensifies this
dynamic by bringing to the marriage a sense of "my family"—which
naturally reminds you of your own childhood.

In raising children, that is, your family experiences as a boy/girl
often remain subconsciously embedded in your memory and define
what's "normal." When you face decisions as a parent, it's natural to
revert to "how Mom and Dad did it" as your default.

Two people raised in different families will therefore have different
ideas about what's normal—and are bound to have conflicts in rearing
their own children together. In order to resolve your differences as a
couple, you need a common focus not only in order to work as a team,
but also to instill security and faith in your children.

Here's where Christian parents have an immeasurable edge on
others: Because we worship the God who creates children, we can see
our children with His eyes and not simply through the narrow lens of
our different childhood families.

Insofar as children are the fruit of "male and female" uniting, that
is, they display God's image. He wants parents to help them do that
by encouraging their faith in Him—as Jesus declares in the opening
verses above.

To center parents in that sacred task, Scripture reminds that your
children reflect your own relationship to God; how you "welcome" the
child reflects how you "welcome" Jesus. In fact, your children remind
you of who you are—or more significantly, *whose* you are, as a child
of God. As they stand before you and your spouse, so as adults the two
of you stand before Father God as His children.

Even as a child cries out "Mommy!" or "Daddy!," that is, so "the Spirit makes you (adults) God's children, and by the Spirit's power we cry out to God, 'Father! My Father!' God's Spirit joins himself to our spirits to declare that we are God's children" (Rom. 8:15,16 parentheses mine; see "The Cry for Daddy" in *Do Pirates Wear Pajamas*).

As John puts it, "To all who received (Jesus), ... he gave *the right to become children of God*" (John 1:12NIV italics mine).

Little boys and girls, that is, teach us adults what it means to be children of God. All of us need that lesson desperately. Even though we ourselves were once kids, as we grow up the world too often promotes the Tree of the Knowledge of Good and Evil, and kidnaps us into its judgments. Eventually, we forget the God we come from, that is, Whose we are—and in that defining sense, who we are.

KINGDOM AMBASSADORS

To Jesus, in fact, *children are ambassadors for the Kingdom of heaven*, reflecting the King of heaven's very presence and the humility required to receive Him. When one nation receives an ambassador from another nation, it's a sign of respect for, and of free communication with the other's country.

How you receive your children therefore reflects how you receive/respect Jesus and communicate freely with the God whose Kingdom Jesus represents. If you don't welcome the child into your life—if you see your child as a distraction or intrusion instead of a blessing—you'll see Jesus as a distraction or intrusion, and won't welcome Him into your life. (see "Can Daddy Come out and Play? The Ministry of the Child" in *Do Pirates Wear Pajamas?*).

Your children are the gateway to the kingdom/place where God rules. So the best way to let God rule your life is to open your heart to your children and let their humility lead you.

Unlike financial planning, therefore, parenting for Christians is not simply about whatever works for the two of you. Rather, Jesus' supremely high regard for children holds us to a standard that's not only higher than, but altogether alien and unknown to the world: Does the way you treat your child make him/her have *greater faith in Jesus*, or less?

Here's a clue to what that means: Jesus healed bodies, cast out evil spirits, died on the cross, and returned to His followers resurrected with God's grace and power for us all. After all that ministry, the central question Jesus asked His disciples—even unto us today—was not, "Will the Son of Man find well-behaved children when he returns?" Rather, it's "Will the Son of Man find faith on earth when he comes?" (Luke 18:8).

The challenge here to Dad and Mom is simple, but ominous for us imperfect adults in this imperfect world: Will we as parents model a trusting humility before God winsome enough for our children to embrace it? That is, will our children, born with trusting and humble spirits, still enjoy that basic aspect of faith after we've been their parents?

Indeed, will we let our children recall us to that faith when we've forgotten it?

That's the task of Christian parenting. It's hard, not only because our sin-nature compels us to control, but because the world itself is infused with a self-centered nature and doesn't often promote humility or trust. Yet that respect for children is what God needs from us dads and moms, so He can access their hearts, and thereby fulfill His purposes in their lives.

You can't instill in someone something they already have. The world tells us that our job as parents is to teach and enforce humility in our children, as via intimidation and punishment. Most often, however, you don't have to teach a child to be humble; they're born that way.

As a parent, you just have to model humility yourself, and thereby bless by example your child's humility—and their faith in Jesus. The Kingdom of God, that is, calls us Christian parents to protect and sustain your children's humility—if only so they can model it for us when we've dismissed it with our pride.

Nurturing your children's faith in Jesus is not about making them obey, but rather, enabling them to trust. For parents, that means being trustworthy yourselves—literally, worthy of your child's trust (see "From Obedience to Trust: From Slavery to Sonship," in *Religion vs. Reality*).

It's a tough task for us natural-born sinners. Nevertheless, you don't have to be perfect as a parent, simply because you can't. In this imperfect world, you will hurt your children. That's why Jesus bears the Father's grace, namely, to replace your self-centered human heart with His heart for your children—even as His heart for you as His child.

Christian parenting is not about whether you'll be perfect or not. Rather, when your imperfect sin-nature leads you to hurt your child, it's about whether you'll acknowledge your sin and ask forgiveness from God and from your child. That's the humility which beckons the Father's heart—and wins your child's heart for Jesus (see "Battling for the Child" in *Fight like a Man*).

Jesus therefore loves children so fiercely because, *like Him, they restore innocence to an awfully guilty world.* The question for Christian parents is simply, Will we let them?

It's good to read the Bible to your children and take them to church to learn about Jesus. But you most convincingly teach your child trust and humility by example. The Good News, meanwhile, is that we otherwise not-so-trusting-and-humble adults have not only the biblical example of faith in Jesus, but the power in His Spirit even today to walk it out.

For starters, you can acknowledge your shortcomings as a parent and ask your children to forgive you when that's appropriate. It's a good example to set if you want your children to confess their own misdeeds.

Still, it's not easy, as any parent knows. In fact, as so often in this fallen world, God confronts us here with a standard which is not only impossible for human beings to achieve, but fraught with serious consequences for not achieving. That's how He gets us to cry out to Him for saving power.

That "millstone" of judgment for falling short as a Christian mom or dad can inspire some serious trembling. Indeed, how do you instill faith in your child—much less have faith yourself—when your child is crying on the airplane or screaming as a toddler in church, dawdling when late for school or stumbling as a student, not to mention chafing as a teenager to scorn your values?

So much for your cherished self-image as the "in-control" mom or dad.

FANTASY OF CONTROL

Here's the point: children will upset your life—but no more than Jesus. That is, they'll upset you *as much as it takes to drive you into the Father's arms for His wisdom and saving power.*

Meanwhile, through the lens of our parental ambitions, it's hard to see your child as the gateway to the Kingdom of heaven. As Christians know all too well, when the standards are high, shame lurks: *What will others think of me—and the faith I represent—when my child is disruptive, uncooperative, disobedient, or under-achieving?*

A child can easily make you feel powerless and inadequate. That stirs shame—and a desperation for "control."

Like unbelievers, too often we Christian parents grasp after a quick-fix control via "discipline" and "obedience." The followers of Jesus, however, would do well to pause here.

After all, any atheist with a big enough whip can control a child. But only a parent with a big enough faith can win a child's heart and *nurture his/her faith in Jesus* (see Ps.118:1-4,).

Before they seek control over their children, therefore, parents who know they themselves are children of God humbly seek His control (see Gal. 5:23). They want most not power to control their children, but rather, wisdom which enables God to control the family.

Granted, it's dicey. You want to be surrendered to God, but not passive. In fact, as in no other human enterprise, in parenting to do nothing can be to do something, even something damaging.

Years ago when I was a Peace Corps Volunteer in West Africa, a local friend of mine told me that he had once visited another area where many foreign missionaries lived. At the market place there one day, he saw a white woman's young child crying beside her while the mother simply went about her business, letting the child cry without any attempt to pick it up or otherwise offer comfort.

That sad testimony of parental abandonment belied any faith the missionaries were otherwise working so hard to instill. "The African mothers at the market were furious," my friend said. "Some were even talking about slapping that woman in the face to make her take care of her child!"

When you're stressed about how to treat your child, your own childhood experience becomes your default. Family loyalty and cultural norms leap into the vacuum—and the beat goes on, generation after generation. We may wish our parents had done it differently, but in the midst of uncertainty and its impending shame, it's natural just to do it how Mom and Dad did it.

HOW A CHILD FEELS

In order to understand how you affect your child, that is, you must know how a child feels. That means you must remember how you felt before your mom and dad. To begin, you need to acknowledge that at some point, your parents' own sin-nature caused them to wound you.

At the same time, you want to forgive your parents and honor them for doing their best. Such grace toward them shows God that you have a humble, child-like heart and thereby moves Him to promise "that you will live a long time in the land I am giving you" (Exod. 20:12).

Ultimately, however, any man or woman with a belly button knows that your natural human wisdom is not enough always to do what's best for your child. It's part of life; we've all hurt our children in some way and need forgiveness.

Too many of us do not know, however, that Jesus is present in God's Holy Spirit to provide the wisdom we need—not only to continue giving our own children what was helpful from our parents, but to forgive and outgrow what was not. "If any one of you lacks wisdom," as James urges, "he should pray to God, who will give it to him, because God gives generously and graciously to all" (James 1:5).

Because the lure of the world is so compelling and even natural, distinctions here are essential.

The kingdom of the world thrives on control, honors order and obedience, and is sustained by performance. The Kingdom of God, however, thrives on child-like humility and is sustained by trust.

If as a child you didn't experience trusting relationship with your parents, such humility is not in your hard drive; it can feel not only strange but vulnerable and risky when you grow up. As a parent yourself later, it's hard to demonstrate humility and trust to your children when you never experienced it yourself as a child. It's easy to fill the gap either by withdrawing passively or punishing aggressively—which can quickly start a fight with your spouse over what your children need and how they "behave."

Thus, a man whose father disciplined him with harsh punishment may either be similarly harsh with his own son, or in an effort to spare his son, balk at any discipline or challenge to the boy's behavior even when it's harmful; a woman whose mother shamed her sexuality may either shame her own daughter similarly, or for fear of hurting as she was hurt, say nothing when her daughter dresses provocatively. (see "Cover up Your Daughter—for My Son's Sake" in *Pure Sex*).

Certainly, a parent's love is not simply about blessing whatever a child does. God doesn't bless whatever we, His children, do. Indeed, in the Bible He denounces certain behaviors. In doing so, however, His Father-heart focuses *not on punishing His children, but rather, saving them from harm.*

Here's what therefore sets Christian parents apart from others: In Jesus, God has defined parental love for us as *wanting the best for His children and therefore empowering them to fulfill His plan for their lives.* That is, He gives us His love so we can love ourselves as much as He does, and therefore make healthy choices for our lives.

Meanwhile, we're responsible to do our best, however imperfect, to conform to His instructions—*not for fear of punishment or being shamed by fellow Christians, but rather, so we can enjoy His protection and the blessing in becoming who He's made us to be.*

Father God demonstrated the essence of such parental love in Jesus' baptism: "This is my own dear son, with whom I am pleased," He proclaimed when Jesus came up out of the water (Matt. 3:17).

What a foundational blessing to hear from your parent!

Yet the Father doesn't give His Son much time to bask in that blessing. Immediately afterward, in fact, the very next verse notes that "Then the Spirit led Jesus into the desert to be tempted by the Devil" (4:1).

NEW COVENANT PARENTING

Here lies the essence of Christ-centered parenting: The Father did not say to His Son, "Go out and fight against evil in yourself and in this world, and when you win, I'll bless you." Rather, He said essentially, "Receive your Father's blessing, and *that* will empower you to win your battles."

As moms and dads, too often our sin-nature gets it backwards. Without trusting relationship with our Father, we retreat into religion. That is, we withhold blessing *until* your child has performed, when in fact, your child needs your blessing first *in order to perform*.

It's called grace. That's the heart of Father God's love for His children and thereby, the hallmark of New Covenant parenting. It's what Jesus made possible for us 2000 years ago and what His Holy Spirit enables in us even now.

Contrary to the world's performance orientation, such Godly love does not require the child's performance—and yet powerfully enables him/her to perform.

In the Kingdom of heaven, it's not about what you do, but about Whose you are. Like Jesus' baptism and squaring off against the devil, your child needs primarily to know the grace of your love in order to battle the world's evil and win (see "The One-Minute Father: Mercy Triumphs over Judgment" in *Do Pirates Wear Pajamas?*).

When you know your Father loves you, that is, you do what He says, because you know it's best for you. That's the holy counterpoint to the world's rebellion—which most children will at some point express as teens, but which your parental blessing is designed eventually to overcome.

Everything else follows: In fact, receiving your Father's blessing makes you *want* Him to rule your life—not for fear of punishment, but for hope of fulfillment (see "From Law to Love," in *Fight like a Man*).

As a parent, you can let God provide that foundation of love by confessing your own need for it and crying out, "Father, please, pour out your love on me!"—like Jesus himself when He "made his prayers and requests with loud cries and tears to God" (Heb. 5:7). As a humble child before Father God, you can surrender your son/daughter to the Father of you both. You can ask Him to show you how to provide what he/she needs—even when you don't have it yourself to give.

When I was sixty and my son a teenager, I visited my dad at his retirement community and tried to impress him with how I was raising my son. "I want to give my son the best," I told him righteously.

"No," he responded wisely, "you want him to *have* the best."

As imperfect human beings, we parents long for *the grace to give our children what we don't have.* That longing becomes sanctified as it drives us into the Father's arms to get it—or at least, as my father implied, to beg Him otherwise to provide for our children what we can't.

We do our best, therefore, but we know the outcome is in God's hands and not our own.

That's faith. It's what Jesus wants us to demonstrate for our children—and what He'll be looking for when He returns.

It's facing the world's sin and evil, even in yourself—and with the humility and trust of a child, crying out to your Father to save you from it. That humble yet determined attitude models a mature, surrendered-and-trusting faith worthy of your children's respect—and the most likely to encourage their faith in Jesus.

MOST AUTHENTIC PRAYER

The most authentic prayer of a dad and mom, therefore, is not, "Give me control over my child," nor even, "Help me give my children what they need." Rather, it's "Father God, give me your heart for this child and make me quick to bless him/her. Show me what you're doing in his/her life and how I can join with you."

That's what your son and daughter need most—indeed, what grows a child's faith in Jesus and enables him/her to face the battles of this world with confidence in His victory.

What's more, as you receive Father God's heart for your child, you'll begin to know at last His heart for you also as His child.

When my son was a toddler, I was praying for him one day and an overwhelming love for him filled my heart. "Father!" I cried out to God, "I can't believe how much I love my son!"

In that moment of joy, I sensed in my mind a simple question: "Why do you love him?"

Puzzled, I hesitated. Certainly, I didn't love him because he performed so well for me—unless you count filling up his diapers and crying at night. And yet, in that holy moment, I knew: "I guess, Father, I love him so much because he's my son."

Yes, I realized. *That's it. Nothing more.*

Even as I basked in the holy glow of that revelation, I was then startled again by another, even more impacting question: "And why do I love you, Gordon?"

I've never been the same since that moment, when I realized that Father God loves me not because I perform so well, but even in spite of my imperfect performance, just because I'm His son.

In that realization, I was freed to love my son as never before. At last, I could ease up on so often telling him to do this or that, and instead, receive and enjoy him—even as my Father God receives and enjoys me (see "Why Do You Love Your Son?" in *Do Pirates Wear Pajamas?*).

As I've done that over the years—though I still struggle at it—my son has grown to trust me more, and I've grown to respect him more.

The surly rebel has left and the responsible young man is emerging, along with his older-and-wiser father!

I need to note here that mine is a dad's story, that parenting can be different for a mom.

In fact, God gives moms a head start on receiving His heart for a child, via the intense physical experience of carrying the baby in her body for nine months and nursing thereafter. Just to be sure, He created the hormone oxytocin in women, which literally bonds her to the baby—even as to her husband in sexual orgasm (see "Sexual Bonding and a Woman's Heart" by Mary in *Pure Sex*).

For dads, on the other hand, the baby-bond is not so physical— nor, in that sense, natural. It must therefore be *super*-natural—even as Jesus modeled in his natural mother Mary and his supernatural Father God.

That means fathering is primarily a faith experience before it's a physical experience. Without the physical bond, in fact, it's easy for a dad to feel inadequate and drop out.

Deliberately meeting and praying with other dads, however, can help a man defuse his shame and gain wisdom by sharing stories together. That's why I pray every other week in my home with two other dads, and variously by phone with three other out-of-town friends who have children older than mine (see "The Wolf Loves the Lone Sheep" in *Sons of the Father*).

The more deliberate a man is about his relationship with Father God and other dads, the more guidance he receives, both natural and supernatural. The more confident a man thereby feels as a dad, the more readily he works together with his wife in parenting the kids. For example, my chapter "Trucks Are for Crashing: Helping Mommy Understand" in *Do Pirates Wear Pajamas?* tells how I was able to help Mary see a major difference between boys and girls and bless our son accordingly as a mom.

SHAME OF INADEQUACY

In any case, feeling inadequate as a parent can stir fights—unless you're both willing to confess you don't have what you need and go to Jesus to get it.

Certainly, popular media beckons children increasingly with its seductive glitter and noise. As parents, we need divine wisdom in order to help our children distinguish the Kingdom of God from the kingdom of this world, which so often distracts from what God is doing.

Thankfully, Father God has provided: "If you don't know what you're doing," James reassures, "pray to the Father. He loves to help. You'll get his help, and won't be condescended to when you ask for it. Ask boldly, believingly, without a second thought" (James 1:5TMB).

Jesus gave His life to restore in us adults such child-like innocence, which opens us to the supernatural wonder of Father God's Kingdom rule. The world's rule, however, is threatened by God's overwhelming power in the spirit realm, and so refuses to acknowledge it. Often, therefore—as in the crucifixion—it destroys the innocence which would welcome God, from graphic shoot-em-up video games for boys to Barbie miniskirts for girls.

The battle for our children's innocence and to encourage faith in Jesus is hard, even overwhelming at times. The world has plans for children and honors their performance; Jesus has reverence for children and honors their humility. The world sees children primarily through the lens of *expect*; Father God sees children through the lens of *respect*.

Sure, it can be dicey trying to show respect for your child while at the same time setting protective boundaries. Again, wisdom is the call here.

Meanwhile, Christian parents must battle not only to protect your children from evil, but to stay focused on God and encourage them toward good. The Father will often suggest His destiny in your children when you see them especially enjoying a particular talent or ability. If God has given them those gifts, you can trust that He will work with you—and with others besides you—to fulfill them.

The Father of us all wants to work together with us to develop those gifts so we can share His blessing with others. Activities like music lessons, homework, and athletic practice require a parent to help the child set boundaries and focus energies—and to reinforce his/ her progress with encouragement.

So bless your children's natural gifting. Ask God for wisdom how to do that without forcing so they rebel and reject it. "Don't exasperate your children by coming down hard on them," as Paul encourages. "Take them by the hand and lead them in the way of the Master" (Ephes. 6:4TMB).

When you exercise a gift from the Father, He feels joy and lets you feel it too, even as a fruit of His Spirit (see Gal. 5:22). As a parent, show your children how much you enjoy their giftings. Cheer at their ball games, high-five a good test grade, read books together and get excited about the story. The Father's joy in you will communicate His encouragement to fulfill it in your child.

TWO-FOLD JOB

To summarize:

Beyond protection and provision, my experience as a dad has led me to believe that a Christian parent's main job is two-fold:

1) to enjoy your child, and

2) to watch for what God is doing in your child and bless it.

That's what Father God proclaimed when Jesus was baptized. He knew He was sending Jesus to save the world. He therefore *not only blessed, but empowered* that mission by declaring He was "well pleased" in His Son.

Such faith and respect makes your children *want* themselves to pursue their gifting and do the work to fulfill it—not because they fear being punished, but because they enjoy the sense of fulfillment.

If it's hard for you to enjoy your child, you likely didn't feel enjoyed by your parents growing up, and the pain from that loss has closed down your heart (see "One Ice Cream at a Time: Growing up with the Child's Help" in *Do Pirates Wear Pajamas?*). Isaiah prophesied that God would send Jesus to "heal the broken-hearted" (Isa. 61:1). Let Him do that for you.

If it's hard for you to see God at work in your child, the baptism of the Spirit will enable you to receive God's eyes (see "Who Is Holy Spirit? Meeting the Active Presence of God Today" in *Broken by Religion, Healed by God*).

In any case, this simple prayer together is a good place for couples to start: "Father, please help us enjoy (child's name). Show us what you're doing in him/her and how we can bless it."

Yes, Father God has plans for us, even uniquely designed to fit each child. And yes, amid His love for children—even those of all ages, even ourselves—God struggles with our sin-nature and our spiritual enemy, which impel us to turn away from Him and frustrate His plans.

So yes, He wants boundaries on our behavior. Not to keep us from having fun, but to protect us from hurting ourselves and others, but to protect us from hurting ourselves and others, to insure that we fulfill His created destiny. Last, but surely not least, the Father gives us free will to honor those boundaries and grow in His purposes—or to reject them, hurt others and ourselves, frustrate His design, and experience the consequences.

BOUNDARIES FOR PROTECTION

God has infused creation with natural laws, such as the Law of Gravity. We're free to honor that reality or not. If you don't—if you step off a cliff—you'll suffer harmful consequences that He does not want for His beloved child.

As with Father God and His Word, you want to let your children know when danger lies ahead, to influence their choices toward safety and fulfillment (see "Captain Donald Duck: Toward New Covenant Parenting" in *Do Pirates Wear Pajamas?*). With toddlers and school-age kids, you have presence and authority to do that. Eventually, however, your child will grow up and look toward leaving home; after that, you won't have either the presence or the power to exercise such authority.

What remains is the trust you've built together over the years. That trust can generate mutual respect, which in turn can mature later into an authority not to coerce, but rather, to influence and even to save.

Years later, you can say to your young-adult son or daughter—as you might to any peer—"Help me understand what you're doing; it sounds to me like it could hurt you." With a history of your respect, that concern can register as loving caution that fosters self-protection, rather than a selfish command that sparks rebellion.

If their womb experience has been peaceful, children are born surrendered and trusting, and in that defining sense, living in the very Kingdom of heaven. Ironically, marvelously, this ultimate goal of life comes with the package from the get-go. *You have to teach a child to distrust.* Sadly, the powers of the world—not only out in the world but in our own sin nature as moms and dads—can do that all too well.

As we moms and dads let Father God parent us in those ways, we learn thereby how to parent our children. When we don't see ourselves as His children and don't allow Him to parent us, we're at the mercy of the world and the enemy as we seek to raise our kids.

As the goal of Christian parenting, instilling your children with faith in Jesus therefore begins with your own faith in Jesus—that is, trusting Him to make you an emotionally safe person for their inborn but fragile trust to grow. Not that you'll always get it right and never hurt them, but that when you do, the heart of the Father in you will not only know, but respectfully ask forgiveness and make amends.

If you've read this far, you may be wondering, When is he going to talk about how to discipline your child?

Actually, I've tried to do that by focusing first on how to let Father God discipline you as a parent and give you greater access to His wisdom. I've offered here a promising, foundational perspective on Christian parenting as common ground for husbands and wives— which can minimize conflict and increase support for each other in parenting decisions.

I hope you appreciate it. Because meanwhile, back at the dinner table, Dad and Mom are arguing over whether to punish their seven-year-old son for yelling at his sister, or to ground their teenage daughter for staying out late the night before.

As so the charges fly between husband and wife:

"Stop criticizing Billy all the time!"

"If you just spent some time with Jenny, you'd see how much she needs you!"

"You've got to quit doing everything for Johnny and give him a chance to learn for himself!"

"You can't let Melissa go out on a date with that guy—he's just no good!"

And so you ask, "Where is this God of surrender and trust when we don't know what to do with our kids?"

As a dad myself, I would simply answer, "He's standing at the door and knocking" (see Rev. 3:20).

ENCOURAGEMENT

Let me close here with a word of encouragement.

If you've read this chapter, I know you want to be a good parent. Like me, I also know that you don't always measure up to your own standard, much less to God's.

Welcome to the human race. We all blow it sometimes with our kids. Hopefully, at the end of the day you learn from your mistakes.

Sure, when you've learned a lesson, you wish you'd learned it earlier. But that's part of growing up in this fallen world, which is never as neatly ordered as we'd like. If you're sincere about being the parents God's called you to be, you'll always be learning. That means you'll be a better parent next week than you were last week.

So don't beat yourselves up for last week's mistakes. Instead, receive the grace God has given you in Jesus. Ask forgiveness, make amends, learn your lessons, and focus on what He's doing now.

And then, press ahead together as beloved children of God in the joys and challenges of growing your children's faith in Jesus.

Growing in your own faith like that means you'll do even better next week.

Other Parenting Resources

Uncertain when I first began writing this chapter, I read Mary the first few paragraphs. Surprisingly, I choked up after a few sentences and turned to her. "We've learned some things over all these years as parents, haven't we?" I managed, then smiled. "I think were ready now to have a baby!"

Our own "baby years" are long gone. But what we've learned from that marvelous season is here, even in this book—and even more so in the heart of the Father who taught it to us and Who's ready to teach you even more.

Here are some resources to help you (All my books and other materials available at http://store.abbafather.com/) :

* *Do Pirates Wear Pajamas? and Other Mysteries in the Adventure of Fathering:* Short stories of how Father God taught me about Himself in being a parent, especially for fathers with sons up to age 12. (paperback, cd/mp3 reading)

Sons of the Father: Healing the Father-Wound in Men Today helps a man recognize how his dad has wounded him, how that affects him as a man, and how Jesus is present to heal him as a dad himself. Includes "Cutting the Cord: A Second Postpartum" and "Beyond Fig Leaves and Cooties: Loving a Woman." (paperback, cd/mp3 reading)

* "Of Fathers and Daughters" in *Healing the Masculine Soul* describes how a girl's relationship with her dad shapes her later expectations as a woman with her husband, and how Jesus heals the father-wound in a woman (dvd/cd/mp3).

*"Battling for the Child: Honor the Boy in You" and "Battling for the Child: Honoring Your Son" in *Fight like a Man* (paperback, cd/mp3 reading)

*Mary recommends the "attachment parenting" focus of Christian pediatrician William Sears and his wife Martha, a nurse—in their book *Christian Parenting and Childcare*.

*Philip Greven's *Spare the Child: The Religious Roots of Punishment and the Psychological Impact of Physical Abuse* is an eye-opening, if not tragic history of how the spirit of religion has often hijacked the Father's heart and caused Christians to squelch their children's faith in Jesus. A tough but essential word for Christian parents. Out of print but available at amazon.com.

* *Dad, Here's What I Really Need from You* by Michelle Watson: a woman's perspective on daughters and fathers.

**Motherless Daughters: The Legacy of Loss,* by secular writer Hope Edelman, shows how the lack of mothering affects a woman and includes a chapter, "The Daughter Becomes a Mother."

Those whose first commitment is to the lordship of Jesus put fewer expectations upon their spouses to meet emotional needs that only God can meet. The lessening of unrealistic expectations gives marriages a stronger foundation upon which to withstand difficult times.[20]

> In marriages, the enemy of God is a pyromaniac who starts fires and makes couples burn against each other; the Father makes couples burn for each other.

10

Fire Prevention

How to Stop a Fight before It Starts

Remember this, my dear brothers! Everyone must be quick to listen and slow to become angry. Man's anger does not achieve God's righteous purpose. James 1:19,20

NOT LONG AGO I RECEIVED a bank notice that I'd overdrawn my checking funds and a $32 service charge had been billed to my account. I confess that I resented the charge. I must also confess, however, that I have a savings account at the same bank; if I had responsibly transferred funds to cover my checking account, the $32 would still be in it.

In a sense, every couple has a marriage account that requires emotional investment. The more you put in it, the more you have available to cover your debts—that is, to withdraw for grace—when the two of you are at odds.

I've talked here so far about when the discussion gets hot. Some fights may be unavoidable, but most can be redeemed when it forces the two of you to face your problem and pray humbly about it together. Nevertheless, couples who are tired of wasting energy on the same old arguments eventually look for ways to head off the firefight before it starts.

Where we live in California, forest fires are not uncommon, and destroy homes. Our local Fire Department urges everyone to clear the dry brush around your property, so when flames threaten they don't reach your house. That's a helpful way to think of marriage conflicts: hidden pain, fear, and shame can be like dead brush around your property that dries from lack of care and catches fire easily to threaten your home.

Here are some ways Mary and I have learned to "clear the brush," spot the flame coming your way, and snuff it out before your home catches fire.

Forgive me if all this seems elementary. But hey, if you and I knew so much, I wouldn't have made enough mistakes to write this book—and you wouldn't be reading it!

1. Listen to each other.

"You never listen to me!"

Ever heard—or spoken—those words before? If you haven't said that, odds are you've thought it as the words simmer under your breath. When the crossfire is heating up, it's easy to be quiet but not really listening; you're too busy plotting how to sharpen your case and waiting for a chance to fire back.

In the opening Scripture above, James offers advice as valuable for marriages now as 2000 years ago, especially for those who—like most of us—have been known to shoot from the hip: If you're in a froth to be hasty about something, be quick to listen to each other.

It's hard. The world doesn't promote genuine listening, largely because that requires being quiet, which can feel weak and vulnerable. Being truly attentive to your spouse takes tremendous courage—the kind that requires surrendering deeply to Father God and trusting Him to protect and lead you (see Ps. 27:1,2).

When a couple come to me for help, therefore, I guide them at the outset in this simple exercise:

"Each of you will have two minutes to explain how you see the problem, while the other person listens carefully without saying anything. When you finish your turn speaking, the other will simply parrot back what he/she heard you say—without any comment or comeback."

SAFETY ZONE

If the "parroting" partner stumbles or "can't remember it all," I have the speaker say it again until the listener can repeat it accurately to the speaker's satisfaction. Then the listener takes a turn and becomes the speaker. Within that enforced safety zone, the speaker is often able to talk more honestly, which enables a deeper level of mutual understanding and trust.

When both partners are satisfied that the other has listened, we go another round: "Now I want you to face each other, hold hands, and take turns telling the other what you need from him/her to help you work together instead of fighting."

When spouse #1 has finished speaking, I ask #2 to parrot back what #1 said, then "say what you're willing to do to satisfy his/her need." Then #2 tells the other what he/she needs and #1 responds.

Even as I write this, I'm dismayed at how simple such an exercise seems, and yet how hard it can be for couples, including Mary and me. Shouldn't two adults be able to do this without a referee?

In a perfect world, sure. But since the Snake talked trash in the Garden, every sports contest needs at least one referee to judge disputes impartially. The black-and-white-striped game official is a badge of lost innocence. In fact, if we could settle our differences so easily, we wouldn't need Jesus!

Nevertheless, Mary and I have learned that healing and intimacy lie within reach if you're willing to fight for it together.

Feeling like the other person doesn't listen to you registers as disrespect, which can stir anger that builds like a powder keg. Here's a thought to help you stay focused: Listen to Father God and don't eat from the Tree of Knowledge: *Surrender your desire to be right for the need to be real.*

Granted, when you're hurting, it's risky to open your heart and be real. But you're in good company when you do it; Jesus blazed that trail on the cross.

Sometimes, a little humor can be good medicine, as it reminds us we're all in this age-old struggle together as men and women.

NOT ABOUT THE NAIL

"It's Not about the Nail," a don't-miss-it, two-minute YouTube skit, makes the point graphically. [21] (Mary showed it to me, so it's woman-certified!)

A man and woman are seated on a couch, turned and facing each other during a heated discussion. The opening scene shows only the lower portion of the woman's face as she looks away from the man, telling him with deep emotion about her "painful struggle" with "this achy…relentless pressure" in her head. After a moment, she turns back to face the man, and we see a large nail in her forehead.

Confused, but straining to be respectful, the man sits quietly. Then gingerly, he notes, "You…have a nail in your head and…I bet if we could just get that out,…you'd be fine."

"Stop doing that!" the woman bursts out angrily. "It's not about the nail. You always try to fix things when what I really need is for you to just listen!"

The man tries to argue his point rationally—but the woman only gets more angry. Eventually, with a measured sigh of resignation, he struggles to accommodate. "That sounds…really…hard," he manages.

At that, the woman breaks into a soft smile at last. "Thanks," she sighs lovingly, putting her hand on his and leaning over with a smile to kiss him.

"OW!," both shout as the nail jams the approaching foreheads; amid their angry voices, the camera fades to the lyrics, "Try to see things my way" from the old Beatles song "We Can Work It Out."

To husbands, let me say here that if you don't understand this, it's OK. You don't need to understand it. You just need to accept it. In a quarrel, for your wife it's not first about fixing her problem, but accepting her feelings.

Just two days ago as I write this, in fact, Mary and I went toe-to-toe over a disagreement in which she felt hurt by something I'd said. Try as I might, I just couldn't get her to see that I had "every reason" to say it. It's embarrassing to report, after twenty-five years of warning other men not to do this as in Chapter 4, but I just wouldn't let go of wanting to be right.

And of course, that only made me more hurtful—and wrong—in Mary's eyes. When we finally got fed up with each other enough to go to Jesus together, I told Him, "OK, Lord, I want to love Mary more than to be right. Please, help me to do that and hear her heart on this."

Eventually, Mary explained how what I'd said had hurt her. With some effort and a great deal of faith, I could say to her, "I can see why my saying that hurt you. Please forgive me."

In the freedom which being real afforded us, she told me that my voice had seemed like a bully. "I don't want you to feel that way," I said, and we talked over some other ways for me to express myself.

Afterward, I was able to say that I felt disrespect from her, and she said she didn't want me to feel that way. When we prayed further, the Father confirmed a "bully" spirit in me and a spirit of "disrespect" in her, which we each acknowledged from our respective family bloodlines. We asked each other's forgiveness and then cast those spirits out.

I can only say that soon afterwards, the light switch flipped, and we were back in each other's arms—basically by acknowledging that we'd always been in the Father's arms but hadn't allowed Him to hold us. Finally, we asked His forgiveness for not receiving earlier that blessing of His care.

"How did we ever get ourselves into *that* one?" Mary asked, as we smiled at each other and shook our heads in dismay.

Well, maybe the Father wanted this story in the book!

In any case, when our Hebrew ancestors in faith set out on their Exodus from slavery, God promised that they would "carry away the wealth of the Egyptians" as a blessing for their suffering and perseverance (Exod. 3:21,22). And so Mary and I came out of the enemy's grip two enemy spirits "lighter," and later that night, with a celebration together worthy of the Father's grace.

At midnight, it was too late for a hotel room with a jacuzzi, but we didn't need it at all. I might note, however, that I booked it in two weeks.

FRUSTRATED COMMUNICATION

Frustrated communication gets funny on both sides of the gender fence.

An old *Suburban Cowgirls* comic strip opens with a woman sitting before a fortune teller.

> "I'd like to make contact with my husband," she says.

> "How long has he been deceased?" the fortune teller asks.

> "You mean I have to wait until he's dead?" the woman exclaims.[22]

And this play on the classic Zen koan, "If a tree falls in the forest and no one is there to hear it, does it make a sound?":

> If a man speaks in the forest, and no woman is there to hear him, is he still wrong?

> If a woman speaks in the forest, and no man is there to hear her, is she still complaining?

Actually, resolving the classic "listen" fight is simple:

Spouse A: You never listen to me!

Spouse B: I know just how you feel! (Just kidding; insert snarky emoji)

Try this instead:

B: That's frustrating. Tell me one more time what it is I'm not getting, and help me understand why this issue is so important to you. I'll try my best to listen.

Done. The door is open. At least, the ball's in A's court now, to respond graciously and honor B's openness and trust. B's job here is to pray quietly, *Father, help!*, and do your very best to be quiet and listen—not just to the words, but to your beloved's heart.

When A has finished, instead of leaping in to defend with your own view, defer to the parrot and *demonstrate that you heard what was said* by doing your best to repeat it—as, for example, "So you're saying that you ....." Wait for a nod or a Yes, and give the other a chance to clarify if necessary.

When you've done your part to listen sincerely, pray for wisdom how, or even whether to respond. Sure, from a legal/50-50 view, it's your turn to speak. But we're talking relationship here, not law. Remember, *it's always God's turn to speak, and when He does, it's a game-changer.*

That is, if you really want it to change.

It's simple respect for the other. It's what you want for yourself, isn't it?

Be bold and show your spouse how to do it. The Father of you both will honor you for it.

2. Keep your language respectful.

> *Do not use harmful words, but only helpful*
> *words, the kind that build up and provide what*
> *is needed, so that what you say will do good to*
> *those who hear you.* Ephes. 4:29

If you're reading this book, you acknowledge that words are powerful.

Respectful language keeps you in the "grace zone," open to each other and to the Father; thoughtless and harsh words just add fuel to the fire and close your hearts in defense.

Even as you censor a word like "frivolous" in talking about money, avoid accusing with extreme, inflammatory words like "never" and "always"—which only box in the other and prompt defenses.

Ban the "d-word" (divorce) and avoid threats, which are just cheap ways to defend yourself. Stay focused on what's bothering you, and trust the outcome to the Father.

Stifle the urge to curse. While four-letter words are included here, I mean something far worse: don't pigeon-hole the other into a negative definition with statements like You're a loser/You'll never amount to anything/You're just like your mother or father/You're immature/ stupid/thoughtless/some other negative label.

A curse like that not only hurts feelings more, but can be a binding judgment when pronounced by someone you love. It can register in your heart as "That's who I am" and even impel you to act like that.

A child whose parents have communicated, "You're a troublemaker," for example, can easily receive that judgment, assume that personality—and make trouble in order to manifest it (see "The One-Minute Father: Mercy Triumphs over Judgment" in *Do Pirates Wear Pajamas?*).

I'm not saying either to ignore or to bless the other's hurtful words and/or actions. I'm saying, Pray for wisdom how to respond—and *don't allow yourself to get hooked into the power that's driving the argument.*

It's one thing to charge, "You're just a thoughtless, self-centered child!" It's another to say, "When you do that it really hurts and makes it hard for me to listen."

Let each of you do the listening—and let God do the judging.

3. Instead of judging, focus on what your spouse did and how that affects you.

Consider this exchange:

Spouse A: You never do what I ask you. You're so thoughtless and unkind!

Spouse B: Look who's talking about "thoughtless and unkind"! You always blow me off when I want something from you!

The racetrack bells ring, the gates fling wide, and they're off and running.

In a circle.

Consider a different scenario:

A: When you don't do what I ask you, I feel ignored and disrespected, like I don't matter to you.

B: Well, you're just too picky.

A: (persevering) When you brush me off like that, it's like you don't care how I'm feeling. That really hurts and makes it hard for me to stay open to you.

Or this:

A: Why do you always pull away when I want sex?

Try this instead:

A: Seems like we've gotten really busy these days. I miss you.

Here's another scene:

A: Why do you have to be so lazy and filthy, the way you just leave a mess everywhere for me to clean up?

Try instead,

A: When the house is clean, I feel fresh and relaxed. I'd appreciate it if we could work together on that.

Consider these other, more general responses:

A: When you talk to me like that, it makes me feel like a little kid. I wish we could just respect each other and talk like adults.

A: When you talk like that, it makes me afraid we'll never get beyond this stupid fighting.

A: When you get angry before we've even talked things over, I feel like I have to defend myself right away. I'd rather be talking about the issue and positive things we can do differently.

A: It's OK, we'll work this out. There's nothing to get angry about. We're just trying to figure out the best way to handle things.

SAFE TO LISTEN

In any case, A's job is to avoid accusation and judgment, stay with what's going on in him/herself, and remain vulnerable until B realizes there's no need to be defensive and it's safe just to listen. It puts the ball in B's court and requires him/her to respond fairly and considerately.

Another word in the Bible for Satan is "The Accuser," as the courtroom term. He likes to keep a couple preoccupied firing accusations back and forth, so they won't stop long enough to see what God's doing. Using "I messages," as A above, instead of accusing or judging the other is a great way to disarm your spouse and focus on the real issue of how the fighting affects you.

Best of all, it gives Holy Spirit more room to work.

If you balk at this tactic, it's likely because it's risky. I understand that you just don't want to get hurt any more. But if your goal is to avoid pain, you might as well stay in bed all day. Life in this broken world includes getting hurt, and healing often requires taking risks.

"In this godless world, you will continue to experience difficulties," as Jesus reminded His followers. "But take heart! I have conquered the world!" (John 16:33 TMB).

Maybe it all sounds to you like a long shot. But after all your short shots have only stoked the fire, it's a promising option. I can testify along with Mary and many other couples, that it works more often than not.

If your partner keeps attacking as you do this, you can say something like, "I know sometimes I accuse and judge you. Please forgive me for that. I don't want to do that anymore, so I'm trying not to do that now. I'm just telling you what's going on in me. I want to know what's going on in you, too. If we can stay focused on that together, I think we can stop hurting each other and get back to loving each other.

"Can we give that a try?"

If the other digs in and still wants to fight, you can say, "I really don't want to waste anymore of our time and energy fighting. If you want to keep doing that, maybe it's better for us to wait a bit and sort things out alone before we talk anymore."

4. Own your "hot buttons."

It only takes a spark, remember, to set off a forest fire. A careless or wrongly placed word out of your mouth can do that. By our speech we can ruin the world, turn harmony into chaos, ...send the whole world up in smoke and go up in smoke with it, smoke right from the pit of hell. James 3:5,6 TMB

Most of us have been wounded by loved ones, both as children by parents and as adults in other relationships. Unforgiveness opens a door in your heart for the enemy to enter and can stir you *to make your spouse pay for what others have done to you.*

"Once bitten, twice shy," as the old saying goes. If a former relationship cheated on you, for example, you can be very sensitive to being hurt again like that and easily become jealous and suspicious, no matter how faithful your spouse today.

Again, if your parents were critical, you learned to protect yourself from any negative comments. As an adult, you may resist facing your wrongdoing and always need to be right—even when your spouse needs you to work together and acknowledge how you've hurt him/her.

Being wounded can feel shameful. But that's why Jesus came, to nail your shame to the cross and free you by God's grace to go openly to the Father for healing.

Instead of projecting onto your spouse your pain from others, dump it onto Jesus—who demonstrated on the cross that He can handle it. Cry out to Him how badly those wounds of the past hurt you. In prayer, focus your pain and anger on the one who wounded you in the past, so you can live in the present and see your spouse as he/she really is (see "Healing Emotional Wounds: Seeing the Past as Jesus Sees It" in *Broken by Religion, Healed by God*).

You can't love a person you don't know, and you can't know your spouse genuinely by looking through the lens of how someone else hurt you in the past.

Brenda, in her late 30's, had never married but was lied to and jilted in her previous relationship. She came to me for help soon after she became engaged to Brad, whom she acknowledged as an honest, trustworthy man.

The previous week, Brad had told her he was going to sign up for an adult education class at 6 pm that night and he would come over to her place afterward at 8. At 5:30, he called her and said that when he went to register, the 6 pm class was booked and he could only get the next one at 8pm. He told her he couldn't see her at 8 as he first said, but would be there later at 10.

PAINFUL MEMORIES

At once, Brenda became nervous as painful memories of her past relationship surfaced. "I knew he was telling me the truth," she allowed, "but when he told me he wasn't coming when he first said he would, I just couldn't get hold of my emotions, the fear that he was lying and cheating. I did my best to settle down and told him how I'd been hurt badly before, that I didn't want that to come between us, but I was struggling not to be afraid and push him away.

"Thankfully, Brad really stepped up," she sighed in relief. "He didn't get angry at me for trying to control him or cave in to my fears and cancel his class. He said it was OK, that he understood and not to worry about anything, that he would come see me as soon as he could after the class."

Brenda smiled. "And that was it. He came over at ten like he said he would, and we had a great time together that night."

Carl's ex-wife had struggled with alcoholism. He came to me soon after he and Carla were engaged. He said he'd taken Carla to a wedding the previous weekend, and when champagne was passed around at the reception, "old memories jumped out of my mind and I panicked."

"I'd worked on my co-dependency issues a lot and thought I'd gotten beyond that," he said. "But I know this is about me, not Carla. She has a glass of wine at a restaurant once in awhile, but that's it.

"I guess my heart's just so open to her that the champagne stirred something deeper from the past that I need to deal with—something that was telling me she's dangerous and to run away from her. I'm fed up with doing that; I really want to stay and work things out together.

"So I screwed up my courage and told Carla that when she had a glass of champagne it stirred some bad relationship memories in me. I said this was my issue and not hers, that I was working on it and would get the prayer and counseling I needed to get beyond it. I knew it wasn't fair to do it, but I asked her if she would give me a month's grace not to drink any alcohol around me during that time so I could get to the root of my problem and take care of it.

NOT YOUR EX

"Carla wasn't too happy about that, I can tell you. She came back flat-out and said, 'I'm not your ex-wife!' I said I knew that, and was sorry to have to ask her to help me like that. But it was all I knew to do, and after a few minutes she managed to say, 'OK, I'll give that to you'."

Over the next few weeks, I worked with Carl to face and pray through that wound from his past relationship, to forgive his ex and let go of her in order to see Carla for herself. Once he had faced those fears openly with Jesus, focused them appropriately on his ex, and received healing for that wound, he could trust the Father with his heart for Carla; his worries about her began to fade away.

"I think that actually, I was using that fear as a way to put distance between us for protection," he said. "I still get scared sometimes about committing to Carla, but now I'm trying to trust Jesus to protect me so she and I can get closer for a future together. I'm ready to go after whatever comes up in me—or in her—that keeps us apart."

When we married, Mary and I had both suffered significant wounds from childhood and past relationships. Soon, we coined a phrase for when one of us would say or do something that triggered those old wounds in the other: "That pushes my buttons."

Simple truth-telling like that brings the issue out from where the prince of Darkness rules and avoids rehashing unnecessary details that would give him a stage. It reassures your spouse that you own your wounds and take responsibility for your healing. Such honesty can short-circuit fears of getting blind-sided into an argument and help you stay focused on the present together.

Of course, if drinking or cheating were an issue for you with a previous partner, your spouse today might also drink or act inappropriate sexually. "Just because you're paranoid," as the saying goes, "doesn't mean they're not out to get you."

Rather than lash back or run yet again, use the pain as an opportunity to seek deeper healing via counseling and prayer, and handle it differently this time (see "'Kick Me' Spirits" in *No Small Snakes*).

5. Pray for wisdom when to raise a difficult issue.

> *But if any of you lacks wisdom, he should*
> *pray to God, who will give it to him; because*
> *God gives generously and graciously to all.*
>
> James 1:5

The entrance to the State Forest near our town posts an eye-catching "Fire Risk" meter-sign, with Smokey the Bear standing above several color-coded options: Low, Moderate, High, and Extremely High.

It's a helpful guide for couples. If your spouse has had a hard day or is otherwise stressed, note the "Extremely High" fire risk; be willing to wait and ask God for wisdom when to bring up a difficult issue.

I know how hard this can be when you're chafing to "express yourself." But patience is a part of love, even a "fruit of the Spirit" (Galat. 5:22). As such, it's a discipline that befits a son/daughter of the Father. English has a word "short-tempered," but no word for "long-tempered," which the Greek word for "patience" means here in the Bible. Hurt feelings can easily be misconstrued and flare into a fight; try to pick a time to talk when the fire risk is low.

It works both ways. If you've had a hard day yourself or are otherwise stressed by events apart from your marriage, take time alone to center yourself and pray for wisdom before bringing up your concern.

Alcoholics Anonymous promotes a helpful acronym, HALT: Hungry, Angry, Lonely, Tired. Be cautious about presenting your case when you or your spouse qualifies as one or more.

You don't have to swallow your anger and pop antacids. Go to Jesus with your pain and anger, and tell Him first how you feel. Instead of being either a doormat or an explosion before your spouse, dump it all on Him. Be real—like Jesus Himself, who "made his prayers and requests with loud cries and tears to God" (Heb. 5:7).

Trust Jesus to listen and give you wisdom when and how—and if—to bring up your issue. When you do, speak your truth with grace: confess that it's hard for you to deal with hurt feelings yourself—and then be patient with Jesus, by surrendering the outcome to Him (see John 1:17).

Sure, it can seem like there's never a perfect time to discuss volatile issues; it's risky no matter how "prepared" you are. But that's where your faith comes in. You won't always do it "right," but Father God always honors a couple who are real with Him and do their best— whether it turns out how you wanted or not.

6. Know when to hold 'em and when to fold 'em.

> *For everything, there is a season, a time for every matter under heaven,...a time to embrace, and a time to refrain from embracing.* (Eccles. 3:1,5RSV)

Sometimes a simple issue can trigger a disproportionate reaction in one or both of you. Be sensitive to when your sincere responses are not connecting and one or both of you is overreacting. When both of you get irritable and you don't see any way to resolve the issue in that moment, be willing to halt the conversation at the top of the hill while you're still civil, before it snowballs down into a fight.

"Doesn't seem like we're tracking on this one," you can say in an even tone. "There's no need to get angry—we're just trying to figure out the best way to do this. Maybe it would be better to deal with it later, when we've each had time to think it over?"

Granted, reason is not always welcome when feelings are simmering.

What, indeed, if you're both angry and can't get centered enough to discuss it with mutual respect? How can you establish some appropriate distance from each other without just stewing in anger and resentment?

Here's a biblical guideline: "In your anger, do not sin. Do not let the sun go down while you are still angry, and do not give the devil a foothold" Eph 4:26,27 NIV.

Biblical faith assumes you'll get angry at times. Being angry is not a sin; it's an emotion. Harboring vengeful thoughts, saying cruel things, acting out harmfully—*those* are sins which anger can stir, and which need to be confessed and forgiven.

So save your spouse the wounding and yourself the time—and shame—by resisting such sinful impulses. Instead, go quickly to your prayer closet with your anger and let the Father prepare you to listen and talk later.

Most armies at some point must retreat in order to regroup and evaluate strategy.

AGREE ON TIME APART

Thus, Paul advises couples struggling with differences in sexual desire:

> Do not deny yourselves to each other, unless you first agree to do so for awhile *in order to spend your time in prayer;* but then resume normal marital relations. In this way you will be kept from giving in to Satan's temptation because of *your lack of self-control.*
> (1 Corinth 7:5 *italics mine*)

"Self-control" is another fruit of the Spirit. Without it, it's easy to get dragged backward into the enemy's merciless pit, where a "lack of self-control" can flood your mind with mean and destructive thoughts (see 2 Corinth. 4:10).

I fact, you do need to retreat: not behind the enemy's defenses, but into your Father's arms. That is, "spend your time in prayer" and seek

God's perspective on the disagreement. Ask Him to search your heart for your part in it and how He sees your spouse.

Sometimes you both need to "agree" on a holy time apart from each other, alone with the Father.

Ordain and empower this time apart by dedicating it to God's purposes. Get real with your Father and tell Him what's making you angry. You may not even know what's making you so hot under the collar; often, the heat of an argument can cause you to misfocus your anger away from its real source. If you try to stuff it down or deal with it in your own strength, the enemy can play you like a piano, stirring thoughts of vengeance and a host of other harmful, mis-directed responses.

You don't have to allow those thoughts to control your mind and heart. Nor do you have to deny your anger and play "nice Christian." Instead, respect your anger as a sign of deeper wounding. Shout out to God instead of to your spouse: "Show me what's going on here, Father!"—and let Him show you the pain which it covers.

During your time apart, beware cooperating with the enemy via compulsive/addictive distractions like drinking, overeating, or binge TV watching. Honor your heart by feeling your sadness and crying when you need to. Talk it over with a trustworthy friend. Amid the pain, try to stay open to Holy Spirit and focused on what God is doing.

I'll give you a hint: He's a good Father. So He's taking care of you. Let Him do that by taking care of yourself.

Sing worship songs. Go for a fast walk. Work up a sweat and take a hot shower. One woman told me that after praying over a fight with her husband, she spent the rest of the day cleaning out her closet, enjoying the memories that long-time-no-worn outfits recalled. She dropped them off at the thrift store—and came out of the argument with a clean closet!

Be willing to step out of your comfort zone. If you can't sleep, get out of bed in the middle of the night and go to your prayer closet. When you go there, pour out your heart to the Father and ask Him what's going on. Ask Jesus how He's praying for you. Command any works of the enemy to be revealed and cast them out.

WHATEVER IS NECESSARY

Tell the Father you're fed up with the foolishness of fighting and hurting the one you love most. Tell Him you'll do whatever is necessary to stop this destructive work in your marriage. Such a humble yet determined attitude allows you to experience *the difference between turning away from your spouse and turning toward Jesus.*

God will bless your taking time apart to wrestle alone with Him for His victory.

Beware, therefore, the world's counterfeit in just leaving your partner as a weapon of punishment.

In the world, the partner with the most credible threat to leave the relationship holds the most power. In the Kingdom of God—as Jesus demonstrated on the cross—the one with the most credible promise to stay and face the issue, even when it's hurtful, has access to the greatest power. That's why each partner needs to be centered in Jesus, in order not to be blackmailed by the other's threat to leave.

That centeredness allows you both to surrender to the Father and trust His timing for reconciliation. You don't need to rush and make up as soon as you sense He's with you.

Respect your spouse's walk with Jesus, and give The Great Physician time to operate on you both while you're apart. If you don't find resolution by the end of the day, then let the sun go down not on your anger, but indeed, on your love for each other and your trust in the Father to reconcile you in His timing.

A "fear of success" can also stir irrational, self-destructive thoughts. If you and your spouse are growing in your love together, your hearts are opening more to each other—even more than in any previous relationship.

Still, something in the past caused your heart to close; if you don't take that old wound to Jesus for healing, it remains to make you afraid when you want to grow beyond it. Often heartfelt thanksgiving and praise can secure the Father's success in your heart and help you overcome past fears.

CURRENT WITH YOUR HEART

Sure, when you're feeling hurt and angry, it can be awfully hard to keep your heart open and thoughts focused on what God is doing. But that's when you need God most. The enemy of God knows that, and that's why in such moments the battle is so fierce for your mind and heart.

The goal here is to stay current with your heart and know what you're feeling, but also to express that wisely. That requires you to be centered in Jesus and trust Him to protect and guide you. "Be innocent as a dove and wise as a serpent," as He put it (Matt. 10:16).

Such faith enables you to keep your lamp lit, expecting the Father will eventually lead you both through this time into His reconciliation. When He does that, you want to be open and "current," ready to celebrate His blessing and not stuck in bitterness from old wounds.

God will bless your taking time apart to wrestle alone with Him for His victory.

Indeed, when you've learned all He wants to teach you from it, He can open the door at last, and you can "resume normal relations."

It's hard.

It's frightening.

Without Jesus, it's impossible.

Because it's war.

In fact, this is the true fight for love—with the power only the Father of you both can provide. If it were so easy, you wouldn't need Jesus to empower you—and He could've saved Himself a lot of trouble on the cross.

GOD'S ANGER

A word about anger here:

When James says, "Man's anger does not achieve God's righteous purposes," he qualifies "anger" as from a particular source, namely, "man's" sinful human nature. In that qualification, he implies another, different source of anger, namely, God's (see "Man's Anger and God's Righteous Purposes" in *Sons of the Father*).

Thus, in the Old Testament, when the Ammonite enemy threatens to destroy an Israeli town, messengers are sent to inform King Saul. "When Saul heard this," the Bible records, "the spirit of God took control of Saul and *he became furious*" (1 Sam. 11:6 italics mine). Another translation says, "the Spirit of God came upon him in power and he *burned in anger*" (NIV, italics mine).

Even as a good father becomes angry when the enemy tries to destroy his children, Father God burns with anger when powers of destruction attack His children covenanted in marriage with Him.

So instead of just reeling from attacks on your marriage and withdrawing into negative thoughts, seize the offensive yourself and fight back. Like King Saul, get fierce and burn with your Father's anger *against the enemy* and not your beloved. Tell God you won't sit idly when the enemy is trying to destroy your marriage—and even using you to do it!

Tell Him you want the victorious power Jesus died to give you, and *He's going to hear from an angry son/daughter until He gives it to you.* Among Jews, in Yiddish such bold determination is called *chutzpah*; in biblical language, it's called faith.

PRAY LIKE JESUS

Show some serious trust in your Father's power and love: Beat on the gates of heaven, like the widow who beat on the judge's door until he granted her request (Luke 18:2): "You've got to show us what's going on here, Father! Give us what we need to win this battle and join our hearts again!"

Last, but certainly not least, pray like Jesus on the night everyone else abandoned him: "My Father, if there is any way, get me out of this. But please, not what I want. You, what do *you* want?" (Matt. 26:42TMB)

Such fierce honesty, surrendered trust, and faithful focus on God will get you where you need to go.

"We want everything you died to give us, Jesus," a couple can pray when you're both ready to go there. "Don't let us get up off the operating table before you're finished. Show us what we need to see, tell us what we need to hear, take us where we need to go, no matter how painful, fearful, or shameful."

Do your best, leave God the rest: "Once again, we give up to you Father, and put our marriage in your hands. Use this time to draw us closer to you and to each other."

Remember, God's definition of peace is simply Jesus: "For he himself is our peace" (Ephes. 2:14). As you press ahead into the battle crying out to Jesus, that means you can trust He's with you *to walk out the victory He's already won on the cross.*

7. Honor the differences between men and women.

This is a profound mystery.... (As Christ loves His Body the Church), every husband must love his wife as he loves (his own body),

and every wife must respect *her husband.*
Ephes. 5:33NIV,TEV, italics mine

Some years ago I had scheduled a couple for ministry who were at loggerheads. The wife Barbara was on time, but explained that her husband Bill, a carpenter, was just finishing a house remodel job and would arrive shortly. In fact, she had just stopped by his work site on the way, and mentioned offhand that she was "really impressed with the beautiful job he'd done on the hardwood floors there."

As she turned to highlight the details of their last fight together, I leapt in. "Wait a minute!" I interjected. "Did you tell Bill what you just told me, how much you liked his work?"

"Actually, I did," Barbara noted—then knit her brow strangely. "In fact, I was kind of surprised at how he lit up with a big smile and said, 'Thank you!' That was the kindest thing he's said to me all week!"

Clearly, she didn't appreciate what she had done for her man.

"Let me put on my man-hat for a minute here," I said. "Working hard at a job and doing it well makes a guy feel like a man. When his wife appreciates that, he receives her compliment as respect. That's what every man wants from his woman; that's why Bill dropped his guard and opened up to you like that."

The Apostle Paul said it long ago in the above Scripture: from her husband, a woman wants most to be loved; from his wife, a man wants most to be respected. Sure, a woman appreciates respect and a man appreciates love. But his love blesses her womanhood and her respect blesses his manhood.

If you want to argue the point, take it up with God and the politically correct police. As Paul notes, it's "a profound mystery." But it's also simple fact—and has been so since before the Bible was written. A woman who respects her husband and a man who loves his wife contribute significantly thereby to their "marriage account."

In today's world, we tend to get it backward. Women may focus on getting respect from men, because they never got it from their fathers or from our often sexist culture. She's stuck in girlhood, waiting for the husband and male-dominated culture to give her a blessing which only Father God can give her as His daughter. "Show me myself the way you see me, Father!" she can pray.

A woman can gain that essential self-respect by receiving His respect for her—which enables her not only to release her husband from that expectation, but indeed, to respect him—and say so (see "Sexual Bonding and a Woman's Heart" by Mary in *Pure Sex*).

On the other side of the coin, a man may complain that "she doesn't give me the love I need!," often because he never got that love from his mother. He's stuck in boyhood, waiting for the woman to give him the love which she needs from him.

To gain security in his manhood, a man must stop demanding love from the woman and instead, go to Father God and get it from the Source (see "Go to the Source for Love" in *Healing the Masculine Soul*). "Father, give me the love I need," he can pray. He can then stop fretting about what "she isn't giving me," receive the love Father God *is* giving him, and enjoy the manly strength in giving it to her. That's what nurtures femininity and enables a wife to blossom as a woman—unto returning that love and blessing to her husband.

It's a blessed cycle: the man loves his wife, which blesses her femininity, which makes her respect him more, which blesses his masculinity, which makes him love her more. It all starts with the Father of them both—and continues as husband and wife do their parts.

LANGUAGES OF LOVE

So what does it mean for the man to "love his wife"?

Certainly, any answer I might offer is trumped by what it means specifically to your own wife. Mary likes the word to "cherish" her (Ephes. 5:29 RSV), that is, to hold her in high value, "to treat with affection and tenderness; to keep fondly in mind."[23]

Paul says that a man's love for his wife is defined by Jesus' love for the Church, that is, a willingness to sacrifice himself for her. While that may not mean literally dying for her, it can well mean sacrificing your determination to defeat her in the argument and surrendering your weapons to repay her for any offense.

At times, it may even mean overlooking the offense and not "reporting" it to anyone but your Father.

Early in our marriage, I discovered the easiest way to find out what makes your wife feel loved: ask her. (What a concept!). When Mary and I married, I simply told her, "I want you to know how much I love you. How can I do to that? What would you do to make yourself feel loved?"

Mary thought for a minute and said, "Well, I'd go and get a manicure."

"I can't cut your toenails for you!" I laughed. "What else?"

Warming to the idea, she didn't miss a beat: "I'd get myself some flowers."

Done. After that, flowers appeared once a week on her vanity table, along with a note telling her things I love about her. That was 1990; those flowers and notes still keep coming today.

Sadly, I need to note here that sometimes a woman herself may not know what makes her feel loved. If so, that most often means she didn't learn how to feel loved as a girl because her father didn't show her. A Christian counselor can help a woman find healing for this wound in her feminine soul (see "Of Fathers and Daughters" in *Healing the Masculine Soul*).

Still, a loving husband can help her know what makes her feel loved by trying different ways to express love to her. A good resource here is *The Five Love Languages*, in which author Gary Chapman describes five major ways love can be communicated: words of affirmation, quality time, giving gifts, acts of service, and physical touch.

Notice which of these registers most convincingly to your wife as love, and do it.

It's not as hard as you think. Most often, your love language is revealed simply in how you express love to others.

Does she offer you compliments and words of praise? Like to spend special time together one-on-one? Give gifts freely? Work to serve others? Give you hugs and back rubs? Whichever of these registers a Yes, do it for her.

Again, wives can learn to show love for their husbands similarly, by determining his "love language(s)."

8. Beware the "re-hash" temptation.

In this fallen world, the enemy may counter-attack and try to regain territory right after you've had a significant breakthrough. Father God may allow this, in order to strengthen your faith and resolve as a couple.

Even after a particular argument has been "settled," you may feel an impulse to bring it up again. You may even think of a new retort you could've used back then that would strengthen your position now.

Beware going there. When those thoughts occur, don't be surprised—and don't follow them immediately. "The flak is thickest when you're over the target" is simple battlefield knowledge. After the fight is over and you've tasted the victory together, be careful and discerning about again bringing up differences you've already expressed.

All too often, the "re-hash" temptation is simply the enemy's bait, preying on your human sin-nature to get you both back in the pit. If you must talk about it still, go first to Jesus and then a trusted prayer partner (see 1 Corinth. 14:29).

If the hurtful behavior that prompted the original dispute persists, ask Jesus how He's praying for you and your spouse (see Rom. 8:34, Heb. 7:25, 9:24). Pray for a renewed measure of wisdom, and surrender your peeve to the Father. Give Him some time to show you His perspective, and let Him lead you.

To head off such confusion, go with God's momentum immediately after reconciling and take the offensive for His advancing Kingdom in your marriage. Turn your focus *from what the enemy is doing against you to what God is doing for you.* Overcome the enemy's "wily ways" with bold kindness: say out loud specifically why you love and respect each other, and praise God for His goodness.

9. Use your authority over your spouse.

Got your attention with that one! Not what you think.

We all want to be blessed by the one we love; genuine love comes with authority to bless. You can choose to withdraw from or exercise faithfully this authority over your spouse, but you can't choose not to have it (see "Use Your Authority for God's Sake" in *Religion vs. Reality*).

Some years ago, a small bestseller *The One-Minute Manager* promoted an embarrassingly simple business strategy: sneak around the office, catch employees in the act of doing something *right*, and tell them.[24]

It works in marriages, too. Make it a habit to spot things you like about your spouse and tell him/her. You'll learn to appreciate each other more—and hearing good things about yourself makes you a good listener!

10. Learn from your mistakes.

There is much we have to say about this matter, but it is hard to explain to you because you are so slow to understand.... Instead of eating solid food, you still have to drink milk. Anyone who has to drink milk is still a child, without any experience in the matter of right and wrong. Solid food, on the other hand, is for mature adults, who through practice *are able to distinguish between good and evil.* (Heb. 5:11-14, italics mine)

Simple experience is one of the most accurate biblical tests for whether going ahead with a word or action is God's idea or not. "Been there, done that!" is the best teacher—though too often, the heat of a fight can spark you to jump back in and say or do the same thing that started a fire last time.

Often, you'll know when a conversation is heading toward those hot buttons, because you've been there before and let the enemy draw you into a fight. Take a deep breath and hold your tongue. Be willing to let a "sensitive" word pass without comment, and pray about it later as the Father leads: alone, with a prayer partner, or directly with your spouse.

Learn from your experience the lessons that expose the enemy's distraction and instead stay focused on what the Father is doing.

11. If the air seems "frosty" between you, consider "checking in" with the other before it freezes.

Sometimes things are said or not said that could potentially trigger an argument. If the air feels a bit heavy or cold between you, should you bring it up and risk unnecessary sparks or see if it goes away after awhile?

Rather than accuse outright or withdraw and simmer, a helpful way to clear the air and separate reality from imagination is simply to ask, "Are we OK?" Taking initiative like that demonstrates there's nothing to fear and can often de-fuse any misunderstanding.

That way, if you need to deal with something, you can do it without an "edge" and diminish chances of an "escalation"—or graciously agree to talk about it later. The goal is to stop embers from glowing hot and flaring up.

Checking in like that can literally cover a multitude of sins.

In fact, her snappy comeback might just mean that her Facebook page for "some frustrating reason" won't come up; his half-hearted welcome-home kiss may simply mean that he forgot to change a word in his book edit before sending it to the publisher (Trust me—it can happen!).

If you ask, "Are we OK?" and the other backs off saying "Yes" too quickly, you may need to be persistent: "If there's something going on, I really wish we could talk about it. I love you and don't want to waste any more time hurting each other." Open the door to communication, but be sensitive and respectful if your spouse needs some time alone to gather his/her thoughts.

12. Don't let the shame of being "wrong" sucker you into a fight.

A: Remember that great salmon dinner we had awhile back on our anniversary in Seattle? I was thinking maybe we could…

B: Actually, we had steak in Seattle. The salmon was on your birthday in San Francisco.

A: No, honey, I distinctly remember we both had salmon at the Space Needle restaurant in Seattle.

B: (firmly): Well, *I* distinctly remember we had steaks there.

A: (exasperated): You always try to change the way things happened from what I say. Why do you always have to be right?

B: (determined): I'm not changing anything. I'm just telling the truth.

A: (feeling cornered; as anger rises, prays quickly with a measured breath, *Jesus, help!*) Whatever—it really doesn't matter. Just saying I'd like to go out for salmon sometime soon. Would you like to do that?

Father God: (impressed) Well done, my daughter/son!

Devil: (depressed) Curses! Foiled again!

13. *And last, but certainly not least:* **(Drum roll, please...)**

   <u>Don't forget to laugh at yourselves.</u>

"Wow! We sure get into it sometimes, don't we?" (cue grinning emoji)

> Great love calls for great courage—
> and great faith in the One who animates it.

11

Caution! I Love Like You

The Case for Grace

> *God puts people right through their faith
> in Jesus Christ. God does this to all who believe
> in Christ, because there is no difference at
> all: everyone has sinned and is far away from
> God's saving presence. But by the free gift of
> God's grace all are put right with him through
> Christ Jesus, who sets them free.* Rom. 3:21-24

SOME YEARS AGO I laughed at a bumper sticker—then had to think again:

CAUTION: I DRIVE LIKE YOU

This gentle reminder of our common sin-nature—and our temptation to deny it—begs a translation for couples:

CAUTION: I LOVE LIKE YOU

"There is no difference at all," as Paul warned; "everyone has sinned and is far away from God's saving presence." This means that both husband and wife are equally self-centered, that both need "the free gift of God's grace" He's given us in Jesus. As *The Message* translation puts it, "Since we've compiled this long and sorry record as sinners (both us and them) and proved that we are utterly incapable of living the glorious lives God wills for us, God did it for us" (parentheses in original).

The first and primary step of healing in a Christian marriage is not righteously letting go of your control to God. In fact, it's humbly confessing that *you never had control of your life in the first place*, and at last trusting the Father for all you need together.

That's real faith.

From there, you're ready to focus on what the Father is doing in your marriage and cooperate with Him. Remember, Jesus did not say, "I will show you the way," but rather, "I *am* the way, the truth and the life. No one goes to the Father except by me" (John 14:6 italics mine).

As my mentor Rev. Bob Whitaker used to say, God's healing is not about doing it with His help, but rather, *letting Him do it with your cooperation*.

In the kingdom of this world, the fight for love focuses on covering your shame and making your spouse give you what you want. In the Kingdom of God, your shame has already been covered by Jesus on the cross, which enables you to receive what God wants for you both, namely, the blessing of His love.

Where God rules, whoever trusts Jesus most—that is, who dismisses shame and cries out for healing first—is the hero. In His Kingdom, the fight is not to change someone else, but rather, to surrender amid your self-centered impulses to God and cooperate with Him to change your own heart.

"Because of God's great mercy to us," as Paul urges,

> I appeal to you: Offer *yourselves as a living sacrifice* to God, dedicated to his service and pleasing to him. This is the true worship

you should offer. Do not conform yourselves to the standards of the world, but *let God transform you inwardly by a complete change of your mind.* Then you will know the will of God—what is good and is pleasing and his perfect will. (Rom. 12:1,2TEV, NIV italics mine)

"Embracing what God does for you is the best thing you can do for him," as *The Message Bible* summarizes this passage.

Sure, as Christian couples, we want the trusting intimacy and fulfillment in a relationship animated by God's Spirit. The rub, however, comes when you discover that your marriage partner is by nature self-centered and prone to turn away from God.

Not a good deal, you think—until you realize that describes you, too.

"Both us and them," as Paul noted.

That means the two of you.

NO HEART A BARGAIN

No human heart is a bargain. Nor does it come with a money-back guarantee. All are flawed and broken before they even come to the store—regardless of how good your parents were or how hard you've tried to be good.

This sin-nature which both husband and wife share feels shameful—which prompts us to hide from each other. Thus, Adam and Eve covered themselves and hid from God after eating the forbidden fruit.

The problem here is not only that you can't hide from God, but that in fact, it's awfully hard to hide from someone you live with (see Heb. 4:12,13). You can't photo-shop the person you wake up with every morning. The closer the two of you become, in fact, the more you see each other's flaws, if only because you suffer the effects.

And that, of course, is what you signed up for when you married. It's the Advanced course in Learning to Love—"for better or worse"— with units on pain and pleasure, wounding and forgiveness, shame and grace.

As your partner's shortcomings become more evident, you can hide from each other and keep a "safe" distance. But if you want the "life abundant" Jesus brings, you need to press ahead together after Father God's perspective—and the risky yet rewarding adventure of His enduring love (see Ps. 118:1-4).

I'm obliged to note, however, that persevering with the Father has a price: you have to stop playing hide-and-seek games and get real with Him and each other. "The heart is hopelessly dark and deceitful," as the prophet Jeremiah warned,

> a puzzle that no one can figure out. But I,
> God, Search the heart and examine the mind. I
> get to the heart of the human. I get to the root
> of things. I treat them as they really are, not as
> they pretend to be. (Jerem. 17:9,10TMB)

The God revealed in Jesus is *after healing, not hiding.* He doesn't enjoy watching us welcome the prince of Darkness by pretending everything's OK and avoiding "the root of things."

Unlike Father God, the enemy can't heal a human heart, forgive hurtful acts, nor save anyone from their sin-nature. Since it can't hide your faults when you live together, it's only hope is to distract from your own sin by focusing on your spouse's instead.

It's an easy sell: create distance by judging and criticizing the other person, and *voila!* You don't get hurt.

If that sounds like a good deal, I have a bridge in New York I want to sell you.

Remember: often the drama in your fights is the enemy's distraction, which keeps you from seeing what God is doing. In particular, the father of Lies makes you see your partner through hyper-critical eyes, and keeps you from appreciating his/her best, God-given qualities.

SPIRIT OF DENIAL

Husbands and wives, please: don't let the enemy steal the "life abundant" which Jesus died to give you both (Jn. 10:10).

Don, for example, had worked to overcome his disappointment and wounding in relationships, beginning with his alcoholic mother. He came to me frustrated by incessant negative thoughts about his wife Donna, and not surprisingly, a loss of attraction.

When we prayed, I heard the words, "It's not about her." As we cried out to the Father for breakthrough, the word "denial" came to my mind; after asking God to confirm it, I shared it with Don.

"Oh, no!" he exclaimed fearfully. "I've thought that for some time now, like I'm in 'denial' about something bad in Donna I don't want to face. I did that as a boy with Mom. I really wanted her love, but she was so up-and-down emotionally that I was scared to get close to her.

"I didn't want to face how broken she was, so I denied it and created a safer, fantasy image of her to love. Do you think I've done that with Donna?"

Rather, I sensed that his problem was not about any flaw in Donna, but in himself. So we thanked Father God for showing us the denial spirit, then asked Holy Spirit for wisdom what it meant. Eventually, we realized that the father of Lies had manipulated Don masterfully.

Like any spouse, Don had seen the best and the worst of his mate. But the enemy had set him against her by making him deny *not her flaws, but rather, the depth of his love for her.* He was afraid to face how much he enjoyed and wanted her.

Don feared opening his heart so unreservedly to a woman and being wounded, as with his mother. Subconsciously, he had bought the devil's offer of "protection" by disallowing his love for Donna and focusing on her shortcomings.

Seeing this pattern, he was relieved—and dismayed at how he'd been suckered into this evil strategy to steal his love for his wife. He asked forgiveness for not trusting God to cover his heart "for better or worse," for not enjoying fully the gift He had given him in Donna. He renounced the spirit of denial, cast it out of him, praised God for bringing Donna to him, and begged for freedom to enjoy the fullness of his love for her.

The next day, he emailed me that he had asked Donna's forgiveness as well. In fact, he had prepared a list of all the things he loved about her and sat down to tell her. The two of them had celebrated God's victory freely and appropriately that night. "It's embarrassing to think how long I've put up with that lying spirit," he said.

Similarly, a woman who was abused or abandoned by her father as a girl often hosts that same spirit of denial later amid a fear of opening her heart to her husband's love.

Here's the takeaway: As with Don, most often *the fight for love begins in your own heart before it ever focuses on your spouse.* It's the battle to overcome your own pain, fear, anger, shame, vengeance, distrust, control, and the host of other thoughts, emotions, and behaviors—not to mention, enemy spirits—which sabotage trusting relationship.

Exposing your heart to receive love can be scary, because it means you're open enough as well to be wounded. As with Don, even success becomes fearful; all too often, you can sabotage your very longing for each other with criticism.

"You always hurt the one you love," as the old song of that title puts it, "the one you shouldn't hurt at all…. You always break the kindest heart with a hasty word you can't recall." [25]

Great love requires great courage—and great faith in the One who animates it.

FANTASY IMAGE

Thus, Jesus was crucified to save us sinful-yet-beloved children of the Father. In modeling such *super*natural love on the cross, Jesus becomes The Way through our wounding unto the Father's heart—and thereby, His healing. As you cry out like Jesus to your Father, that is, He resurrects your broken spirit by replacing it with His Spirit.

In such grace, you can not only forgive, but bless each other as well. That's the marriage of mercy and grace.

That's how God, and not the enemy, gets the final word.

It's how Mary's and my "Fight of fights" at the beginning of this book led to love-making.

Father God's love is not about fairy tale images of your spouse that reassure you won't get hurt. But neither is it about *holding negative thoughts of your spouse to justify your fear of intimacy.* It's about renouncing such denial and seeing the other genuinely, with God's eyes—sin-nature and all, "for better or worse"—and pressing on together in the fight for love. That's how you respect, protect, and celebrate the love God has given you for each other, and trust Him to shepherd it.

Followers of the crucified Christ know that such genuine love comes with a cost, even self-sacrifice on the other's behalf. Laying your mask at the cross can be terrifying as you release all those false images of yourself and your spouse—until you realize they only "protected" you from the intimacy you long for.

Those who persevere in this holy battle discover thereby the reward of genuine intimacy: not just healing, but indeed, the new and resurrected life we're made for, even together.

Being so real with God and each other is hard and fearful work, but trust me: it's easier than suffering those fights that last into the night and beyond. Our "Fight of fights" may have been necessary for God to get our attention, but Mary and I were determined after that to learn our lesson.

When it's harder to stay up than to make up, you're ready to grow up.

Nobody wants to get hurt, and nobody can hurt you worse than the person closest to you. But in the crucible of that wounding, the power of the world meets the power of God, where both death and resurrection mingle.

Amid such authentic, transforming love, you "fall" in love not first into your spouse's arms, but into your Father God's arms. It's not about trusting the other never to hurt you, but rather, trusting your Father always to be with you, that is, to use your broken-open heart as an avenue to His heart.

Like Adam and Eve, in the beginning we were all innocent children, freely open and trusting—until the powers of the world wounded you enough to close your heart in protection. As an adult, opening your heart again, as when you were a child, often means facing and working through those old pains and fears that originally made you close it. As a child, your nervous system wasn't capable of processing such pain. But now, as an adult, you can revisit that crippling wound with Jesus and let Him heal it.

BE GENTLE

So be gentle with yourselves and receive your Father's healing. Beware the enemy's ploy to steal it by charging that "You don't deserve God's goodness." Of course you don't deserve it; what could we possibly do to earn Jesus' dying for us? *If life were about what we deserve, we'd all be toast.*

212 Love to Fight or Fighting to Love?

Don't bother trying to justify yourself; instead, just praise Jesus for "the free gift of God's grace in Christ Jesus." In fact, the more you receive His healing grace, the more of it you have to give your spouse.

"Forgive me, Father!" we can cry out ever since Jesus, with confidence not only that He will wipe all record of our sin away, but bless us far beyond our deserving. "As far as the east is from the west," the Psalmist declares,

> so far does he remove our sins from us.
>
> As a father is kind to his children, so the
> Lord is kind to those who honor him.
>
> He knows what we are made of, he
> remembers that we are dust. (Ps. 103:12-14).

A healthy father enjoys giving to his son or daughter. In order to enjoy giving new life to us, Father God had to make us worthy to receive it. That's why Jesus was crucified, to pay the debt of our sin-nature for us and restore us as His sons and daughters. That love allows us not only *to receive His blessings, but in turn to bless others—even your spouse*.

No one is more amazed by a gift than someone who doesn't deserve it.

The only question is, will you receive it?

Father God will teach you and your spouse about His love—in particular, about forgiveness and grace—via your conflicts. As you experience thereby the fruit of Holy Spirit's healing, receive it by together thanking God for your love as a free and undeserved gift..

Praise your Father and thank Him for overcoming your sin-nature and releasing you to love each other more deeply. Determine to press through your conflicts together and trust Him to bless your efforts—and turn your mistakes into precious lessons.

We don't always get it right, you know. But if we're real before God and each other, He can make it right.

So lay your pride at the cross. Send your shame to hell where it belongs, and start talking together faith-full-ly about your pains and fears, your hopes and joys. *Stay focused on what the Father is doing and seek His Spirit's power to join Him.*

As you give more room for Him to work like this, the "fruit" of His Spirit will grow in your marriage: "things like affection for others (love), exuberance about life (joy), serenity (peace)," as Paul declares, and then continues,

> We develop a willingness to stick with things (patience), a sense of compassion in the heart (kindness), and a conviction that a basic holiness permeates things and people (goodness). We find ourselves involved in loyal commitments (faithfulness), not needing to force our way in life (gentleness), able to marshal and direct our energies wisely (self-control). (Galat. 5:22,23 TMB, parentheses NIV).

Again, these blessings are "fruit"; they appear and grow *not by your human effort, but by the Father's grace via your surrender and trust.*

READY THE ROAD

Sure, there's work to be done: a farmer needs to cultivate the soil, plant the seed, and protect the crop. But no farmer, no matter how dedicated, can make a tree grow or cause fruit to appear. Farmers work hard to keep the tree healthy—and trust God for the crop.

Similarly, there's work to be done for husbands and wives. That's what John the Baptist meant when he announced that Jesus was coming: "Get the road ready for the Lord; make a straight path for him to travel" (Mark 1:3).

What does that mean for your marriage?

It doesn't mean running out and trying to "find Jesus." Rather, it means realizing that *He's looking for you*, jealous of the world to win your heart. He wants to come into your life and your marriage. The more you both clear a "straight path" for Him to do that—by fighting in Holy Spirit's power against your self-centered sin-nature and the destructive schemes of the enemy—the more access He has to your hearts.

And so we fight hard, even desperately, to overcome your pain and fear, and keep your marriage healthy—but we trust the fruit/ outcome to God. We persevere with Him, as at last we realize—both fearfully and gratefully—that in this fallen world, ultimately *we have no other place to go for healing but to the Father.* In fact, until you go to Him broken, spent, and lost, all your human efforts to save yourself eventually fail; worse, they distract you from God's purpose in your life together and His power to fulfill it.

Thus, Jesus promised His followers that "the world will make you suffer." At the same time, however, he encouraged us amid the struggle, "But be brave! I have overcome the world" (John 16:33).

To paraphrase Jesus here, in this fallen world Christian husbands and wives can expect to struggle together—if only because that fallenness lives in you both. But we can also trust that when you surrender yourselves to Father God, the fruit of His Spirit will appear in the season of His timing, because *the battles you fight together have already been won by the world's Savior*—and yours.

Often fighting reveals how self-centered and petty we can be. By surrendering to Jesus, however, a couple can learn the humility which allows Him to overcome our sin-nature and enable enduring love (see Ps. 118:1-4).

SUPERNATURAL LOVE

Let's face it: a love which unites two unique human beings of different family backgrounds and emotional languages "as long as we both shall live," can only be supernatural. None of us human beings have that kind of love by nature. But since Jesus, that's no excuse—only an occasion to go to Him and get it.

We all live in a fallen world among other fallen human beings. Marriage is the sanctuary wherein painful battles against your sin-nature and the enemy drive you into the Father's arms.

Surrendering to the Father gives His Holy Spirit more room to work freely in your life—the very Spirit, in fact, who animates Jesus and therefore lives among and within faithful Christians today.

In that sense, marriage is a house that your Father has built for the two of you in His Kingdom and is inviting you now to live in together—a home, in fact, that will rise mightily before the world's destruction precisely insofar as a husband and wife fall humbly before Him.

The takeaway here is simple, but oh-so-hard for our ingrown human nature: *The more the two of you surrender to Jesus, the more freely you walk in the Father's victory together and fulfill His created purpose for your marriage.*

Such sanctified surrender changes everything. In the kingdom of the world, winning an argument is an esteemed goal for your glory; in the Kingdom of God, it's an unholy distraction from His glory—and from His healing.

So here's even more Good News: As you welcome Jesus and the Father's Kingdom rule into your life together—wonder of wonders!—love, which amid the fight seemed so distant, begins to grow—and show. One evening, you gaze at your beloved across the dinner table, and find yourself shaking your head in awe, thinking, *Thank you, Father!*

And later after dinner, in a quiet moment when it's just the two of you, you talk about how grateful you are to be together.

As a grateful husband, I like to think that's what the Apostle Paul had in mind when he wrote,

> Let us continue to love each other, since love comes from God. Everyone who loves is born of God and experiences a relationship with God.... God is love. When we take up permanent residence in a life of love, we live in God and God lives in us. This way, love has the run of the house, becomes at home and mature in us. (1 John 4:7,16TMB)

May the two of you be so blessed.

"Father," he said,

"I'm grateful for this woman

you have given me to love."

"Father," she said,

"I'm grateful for this man

you have given me to love."

Because now you know:

It's not hard for you to love each other.

It's impossible for you—

but not for Me.

Because love is who I am.

That's why I promise—and warn—you both:

"You have no chance at all

if you think you can pull it off yourself.

Every chance in the world if you trust God to do it."

Matt. 19:26 TMB

Afterword

IN ORDER TO SEE the spiritual battle for marriages in perspective, let me summarize here the general progression which Mary and I most often follow in resolving our differences. It's not always this neat, but note the takeaway: it all hinges on surrendering humbly to Father God and trusting Him for the outcome:

1. Feeling hurt by or disagreeing strongly with something the other has said or done.

2. Getting defensive and angry at each other in order to cover a fear of being shamed or hurt more.

3. Reaching a point of such frustration that any further listening, talking, or silently fuming only increases the pain and anger.

4. One of us asking the other, "Can we pray together?"

5. Joining hands and each thanking God for our marriage, *asking His forgiveness for turning away from each other instead of toward Him,* declaring that we don't want to waste any more time fighting, and begging Him to come by the power of His Spirit and lead us into healing.

6. Each praying, "Father, tell me whatever I'm doing that's hurting (the other), and give me the grace to listen."

7. Listening to each other's grievance, asking forgiveness, and forgiving

8. Asking Holy Spirit to identify any evil spirits in either or both of us—or attacking from outside us—which have been fueling the conflict (and might continue to do so afterwards)

9. Casting those spirits out of either or both of us in the name of Jesus, and asking the Father to replace their destructive work with a positive counter-working of His Holy Spirit.

In this book, I've focused on steps #1-7, but only hinted occasionally about steps #8,9 and spiritual warfare. Hopefully, I've done so credibly for those who want to engage more deliberately in that battle later for deeper healing.

As Scripture assures, Jesus has come "to destroy the works of the devil" and provided Holy Spirit's knowledge, wisdom, and discernment to lead us in His victory. Yet until He returns, our sin-nature will remain to confuse if not mislead us. "We don't yet see things clearly," as Paul puts it. "We're squinting in a fog, peering through a mist" (1 Cor. 13:12 TMB).

In dealing with the enemy, therefore, a healthy caution is in order.

Before talking explicitly and thoroughly about the powers of evil, it's best to lay a foundation in Holy Spirit's power to heal the emotional wounds and check the sinful impulses which most often sponsor the enemy's work. Not dealing with these root issues in your life will compromise your spiritual armor.

That's why I didn't include a more comprehensive study of battling against demons in this book. We're all human enough to seek a quicker fix than genuine healing might allow; it's tempting to leap ahead and begin casting out spirits without being properly grounded in the Father's healing and protection.

I don't want to make it easy for readers to do that.

And so Mary and I have done our best herein to help you build that foundation. After you've done that with this book, you can pray together and ask the Father if He would have you focus on more specific works of the enemy and spiritual warfare strategies.

If so, the resources listed below will help you do that:

RESOURCES

- *A Couples Guide to Spiritual Warfare,* my follow-up booklet, exposes particular spirits which most often attack marriages and teaches how to evict them.

- *No Small Snakes: A Journey into Spiritual Warfare* offers a more advanced, comprehensive treatment via my personal story of how I first met the enemy and learned to overcome its schemes in the power of Holy Spirit.

- *Religion vs Reality: Facing the Home Front in Spiritual Warfare* focuses on overcoming specific works of the enemy which undermine God's work today, often among Christians.

- *Deliverance from Evil Spirits,* by Francis MacNutt, a pioneer in the charismatic movement, offers a balanced view of spiritual warfare.

- *A Handbook on Holy Spirit Baptism,* by Don Basham, will enable you to receive the baptism of the Holy Spirit, and thereby, initiate you into the supernatural worldview which infuses biblical faith.

"Well, honey, the book's done at last!" he sighs. "I like it. In fact, I think I learned a few things myself in writing it."

"That's true," she says, smiling mischievously. And then, drawing closer with a warm hug and kiss, she adds, "You're a lot nicer since you wrote it!"

"*What?*" he exclaims, tickling her as they both laugh.

Later, that night, ... but wait—no need to tell you where this is going.

About the Authors

Gordon Dalbey's widely acclaimed classic *Healing the Masculine Soul* helped pioneer the men's movement in 1988 and remains a bestseller today, with French and Italian translations. A popular speaker at conferences and retreats around the US and world, he has ministered in England, Hong Kong, Australia, New Zealand, Italy, France, Switzerland, Canada, and South Africa. A former news reporter (Charlotte NC), Peace Corps Volunteer (Nigeria), high school teacher (Chicago, San Jose CA) and pastor (Los Angeles), he holds an M.Div. from Harvard Divinity School, an M.A. in journalism from Stanford, and a B.A. from Duke.

The author of nine books, Gordon has appeared on *Focus on the Family* and many other radio and TV programs. His magazine publications include *Reader's Digest, The Los Angeles Times, Catholic Digest, Leadership Journal, Christian Century*, and *New Man*.

Mary Andrews-Dalbey holds a PhD in Professional Psychology, MS in Psychiatric Nursing, and a BS in Nursing. She has been a pediatric and psychiatric nurse, Christian counselor, and director of a ministry to pregnant, unwed women. She now counsels at-risk families for a child-abuse prevention agency. Mary has spoken internationally at women's conferences. Her book *The REST of Your Life, Discovering God's Rest in a Driven, Demanding, Distressful World* portrays how true rest is not about our doing less, but rather, trusting God to do more. Her psychological and medical and backgrounds, plus her ministry leadership experience, have given her a unique approach to healing from a spiritual, emotional, and physical perspective.

Other Gordon Dalbey books

paperbacks, audio cd/mp3 at www.abbafather.com

ebooks at www.kindle.com

Both refreshing and upending, Gordon Dalbey's books for men take us to depths of authentic manhood where we're humbled by its mystery and engaged by its call. Apart from either violence or lust, these books restore both courage and passion to manhood. Here's a masculinity you can trust—and the Father who makes it happen.

Healing the Masculine Soul

Today, politically correct voices cry out for men to be more sensitive, to tame our masculine nature. Meanwhile, the media bombards us with "macho" images of violence and lust. Is it any wonder men today are left bewildered about what manhood really is?

This pioneering, bestselling classic gives men hope for restoration by showing how Jesus enables us to get real with ourselves, with Him, and with other men. Its refreshing journey into the masculine soul dares men to break free from deceptive stereotypes and discover the power and blessing of authentic manhood.

Sons of the Father

Healing the Father-Wound in Men Today

"When you became a dad for the first time, did your own dad reach out to you with support, encouragement, or helpful advice?" Out of 350 Christian fathers, only 5 hands went up. "When you were 11 or 12, did your father talk to you about sex and relating to women?" I asked another gathering of 150 Christian men. Two hands.

Men today suffer a deep father-wound, which has left us unequipped for manhood. The father of Lies capitalizes on its shame and blackmails us into isolation, denial, and a host of bogus cover-ups—from money and guns to alcohol, sex, and performance religion.

The true Father of all men has come in Jesus to draw us back to Himself and to the man He created you to be. Here's the map to get you there.

Fight like a Man

A New Manhood for a New Warfare

9/11 revealed the enemy of God and humanity as rooted in shame-based religion. The focus of warfare has now shifted dramatically from military battles to the hearts of men.

This trail-blazing book focuses on the crippling byproduct of fatherlessness in men today, namely, shame—too often fostered by religion, always overcome by Jesus. It's not about how to be a man, but knowing the Father who rescues and restores men. It's not even about how to be a warrior, but surrendering to the Commander of the Lord's Army.

Here, you won't be exhorted to obey, but invited to trust. You won't be commanded to do it right, but freed to be real. You won't be warned to be strong, but promised your Father's strength as you experience the grace and dignity of being His son.

The awful wounding of our times, from family breakups and sexual confusion to drugs and violence, has left us hungry for a faith that embraces reality as graphically as we're forced to in this increasingly lost and broken world.

Do Pirates Wear Pajamas?

And Other Mysteries in the Adventure of Fathering

"Daddy, it's not an adventure unless it's a little scary!"

The lessons of fathering are the character of God.

Watch for what God is doing in your child, and bless it.

In these impacting, real-life stories, you'll meet a bestselling Christian author who's a dad in on-the-job training—sometimes stumbling, sometimes celebrating, always learning. Experience teaches us the best lessons. But too often, we men miss the experience because we fear the shame of not knowing how to do it.

There's good news here for us dads: We're in this adventure together as men, and the Father of us all stands with us. You don't have to know how to do it. You just need to know Who does it—and trust Him to give you what you need to be the dad your child needs.

> **The awful wounding of our times, from family breakups and sexual confusion to drugs and violence, has left us hungry for a faith that embraces reality as graphically as we're forced to in this increasingly lost and broken world.**

No Small Snakes

A Journey into Spiritual Warfare

This is my upending personal story of meeting and learning to overcome the powers of evil as portrayed in the Bible.

The problem in confronting spiritual reality, I discovered, is not that our childish imagination gets hooked into foolish fears, but that something real is evil and we can't control it. This humbling truth stirs shame in our Western, control-oriented culture and we deny the reality of supernatural evil. But pretending there's no thief in your house doesn't protect you from being robbed; it only gives thieves free rein to steal whatever they want.

In Jesus, God has invited us to exchange the illusion of our control for the reality of His power. This book extends that invitation to you.

Broken by Religion, Healed by God

Restoring the Evangelical, Sacramental, Pentecostal, Social Justice Church

This is my story of how I became born again among Evangelicals, discovered the sacrament among Catholics, was baptized with Holy Spirit among Pentecostals, and transformed by social justice ministries among Oldline Reformers. But it's also about the crippling brokenness in the Body of Christ today, which that journey revealed—how the Church has divided itself by these four very ways people meet Jesus, sabotaging its credibility and mission.

The same spirits of shame and division which animated the Pharisees and 9/11 terrorists have for centuries distracted Christians from what Jesus is doing and kept us from seeing each other as He does. Here's how to join Jesus as He battles unto today to heal His broken Body—and through it, this broken world.

Religion vs Reality

Facing the Home Front in Spiritual Warfare

Go figure out what this scripture means: "I'm after mercy, not religion. I'm here to invite outsiders, not to coddle insiders." (Matt. 9:13,14TMB)

Since Jesus, religion is obsolete.

Religion is our human effort to cover the shame of our sin-nature.

Honest human beings know it doesn't work. In fact, that's why Jesus came—not to cover our shame but to remove it. He thereby revealed religion as a tool of the enemy to distract us from His work.

The power of evil unmasks this false security of religion. And so our sophisticated Western pride denies the reality of evil because it reminds us we're not in control. Tragically, we thereby forfeit the power to overcome it.

Here's how to reclaim that power.

Chapters focus on works of the enemy often hidden by popular culture and religious denial. Titles include Facing Spiritual Denial, 9/11 and the Spirit of Religion, Ball Games and the Battle for Men's Souls, Homosexuality and the Father Wound, White Racism and Spiritual Imperialism, Unmasking Halloween, Overcoming Depression, and Delivered from Abortion.

Gordon Dalbey's books will stir you to a faith both passionate about its truth and compassionate in its grace. Here's freedom from universal tolerance on the one hand and narrow condemnation on the other—and Jesus at work today as God's vital Third Option to the world's self-defeating enmity.

Pure Sex

The Spirituality of Desire

with Mary Andrews-Dalbey, Ph.D.

There's more to sex than mere skin on skin. Sex is as much spiritual mystery as physical fact. 1 Corinth. 6:16,17TMB

Today's quest for "sexual freedom" has misled us into a vast wilderness of options where we've forgotten what sexual desire is, where it comes from, how it was designed to function, and where the power comes from to fulfill it. Christians, meanwhile, have banned sexuality from church, leaving a vacuum which the world is literally hell-bent to fill. "Sex is dirty and immoral," as the culture confounds, "so save it for marriage and the one you love most!"

Here's the trailhead to authentic sexual freedom: not the absence of restrictions, but the presence of Father God, who enables its authentic fulfillment. Chapters include Sex as Holy Nostalgia, The Genesis of Modesty, Homosexuality and History: A Perfect Storm, Spiritual Consequences of Sexual Union, Sexuality and Religion: A Marriage Made in Hell, Controlling Uncontrollable Desire, Was It Good for You (Too)? Sexual Bonding and a Woman's Heart (Mary Andrews-Dalbey PhD).

A Couple's Guide to Spiritual Warfare

For couples committed to fighting together against their common, spiritual enemy, here's how to identify specific spirits which most often attack marriages and how to cast them out.

The REST of Your Life

Discovering God's Rest in a Driven, Demanding, Distressful World

By Mary Andrews-Dalbey, PhD

We're tired. We're stressed. We're over-extended. But we can't stop. Too often, we stay busy in order to make ourselves acceptable and cover up a sense of shame and inadequacy. At the end of creation, God rested—not because He was tired, but because He was finished. Likewise, we can surrender to His finished work on the cross and enter His Sabbath Rest. The rest God offers does not require the luxury of a settled life, but rather, the comfort of a secured soul that trusts and relies on Him. The Sabbath, therefore, is not about what you don't do, but about what God does; not about your doing less, but about trusting God to do more.

Formatted as a 10-week workbook for groups, this book will teach you, even in the midst of our daily responsibilities, how to find security and serenity as He's working in your life.

NOTES

1   Barbara Lewis, "Come Home," Atlantic Records, 1964.

2   *Uncle John's Great Big Bathroom Reader* (Ashland, OR: The Bathroom Reader's Press, 1998), 103.

3   https://www.barna.com/research/new-marriage-and-divorce-statistics-released/

4   I found this insight in a statement by author Rev. Susan Miele, but cannot remember where.

5   *Prager, Dennis. "Judaism's Sexual Revolution: Why Judaism (and then Christianity) Rejected Homosexuality," Crisis, vol. 11, no. 8 (September 1993).* http://www.orthodoxytoday.org/articles2/PragerHomosexuality.php. *Regarding homosexuality, Prager adds,* "Even if the majority of men became incapable of making love to women, it would still not be normal. Men are designed to make love to women, and vice versa. The eye provides an appropriate analogy: If the majority of the population became blind, blindness would still be abnormal. The eye was designed to see."

6   *Tanya Tucker Love Songs* (cd), "Strong Enough to Bend." Beth Nielson Chapman and Don Schlitz, BMG Songs, Inc., 1995.

7   *The Wittenburg Door*, Dec 84-Jan 85.

8   David and Vera Mace, *How to Have a Happy Marriage* (Nashville: Abingdon, 1980).

9   Boyd, Greg. *Repenting of Religion* (Ada, MI: Baker Books, 2004).

10   Bridges, Jerry. *Respectable Sins: Confronting the Sins We Tolerate* (Colorado Springs: Nav Press, 2007).

11   Joyner, Rick. *There Were Two Trees in the Garden* (Charlotte, NC: Morning Star Publications, 1986), p. 8.

12   Willie Nelson, "If You Could Touch Her at All" (RCA Records, 1978).

13   Belinda Luscombe, "Porn and the Threat to Virility," *Time*, 4/11/16, p. 49.

14 http://www.childmolestationvictims.com/child-molestation-sexual-abuse-statistics/

15 Robin Mark, "Not by Might," Daybreak Music, 1998, in cd *Come Heal This Land* (East Sussex, UK: 2001)

16 Lawyer John Thyden in Jeff Wuorio, "Money and Marriage Issues: The New Rules for Couples," *Good Housekeeping Magazine*, 4/11/08.

17 *Santa Barbara News Press*, 7/20/16, B4.

18 "Do the Manly Thing," Dave Ramsey, *Santa Barbara News Press*, 4/2/17, p. F1. "That extra cash …is for the good of your family," Ramsey advises the writer. "(It's not) that I get to play more because I work extra, while the rest of the family suffers."

19 Michael Howard, "How to Stop Fighting with Your Spouse about Unnecessary Spending," https://nortonsafe.search.ask.com/web?geo=en_US&prt=&ctype=&o=APN11910&chn=&ver=&tpr=5&q=How+Couples+Should+Talk+About+Unnecessary+Spending&ots=1461440858357,10/9/15

20 https://gotquestions.org/Christian-divorce-rate.html

21 https://vimeo.com/66753575.

22 Janet Alfieri and Ed Colley, *Suburban Cowgirls* (1990-95). I neglected to note the date on this particular strip.

23 The *American Heritage College Dictionary* 4th Edition (Boston: Houghton Mifflin), 2004, p.247.

24 Kenneth H. Blanchard and Spencer Johnson, *The One Minute Manager* (2003).

25 Universal Music Publishing Group, Sony/ATV Music Publishing LLC

Made in the USA
Columbia, SC
10 December 2017